BOB MANGAT

The Automated Entrepreneur:

How to Boost Sales, Maximize Profits, & CRUSH the Competition

Systemize – Optimize – Monetize Your Business on Autopilot!

ISBN-13: 978-0-9970968-1-1
ISBN-10: 0-9970968-1-0

This publication is designed to provide accurate and authorita-
tive information in regard to the subject matter covered. It is sold
with the understanding that the publisher is not engaged in ren-
dering medical, legal, accounting, or other professional services.

Published by: Celebrity Expert Author
http://celebrityexpertauthor.com

Canadian Address:	US Address:
Celebrity Expert Author	1300 Boblett Street
501- 1155 The High Street,	Unit A-218
Coquitlam, BC, Canada	Blaine, WA 98230
V3B.7W4	Phone: (866) 492-6623
Phone: (604) 941-3041	Fax: (250) 493-6603
Fax: (604) 944-7993	

Contents

Contents

PREFACE

You're tired of no longer bringing in the same profits that you garnered as a new business owner—or maybe you are looking to get started as an entrepreneur, but you don't have the direction that you need right now. You have yet to discover a single strategy that works best for you and your business, let alone one that supports your ideal lifestyle—and you're probably not happy about putting in so many hours and getting so little in return.

Believe it or not, running a successful business isn't about finding a single winning strategy. Instead of searching endlessly for *that one perfect strategy* that will invigorate or revive your business, let's use the principles in this book to craft a multi-pronged strategy that will address every aspect—not just one—of what makes your business work. You can't keep relying on referrals and refusing to use any type of marketing tools; it's time to change your old assumptions about how business works and open your mind to what *really* works for every business owner: from the day that you launch your business to the day that you sell it—and beyond!

Fortunately, this book that you have in your hands (or are viewing online) is precisely what you need in order to break away from the status quo, which will enable you to boost sales, maximize profits, and CRUSH the competition! This "NO B.S."

business playbook will coach you on a variety of proven strategies to not only create wealth, but to also enjoy the stress-free freedom that comes from envisioning, creating, and finally living your own ideal lifestyle.

You aren't considering buying yet another business book that will be skim-read and then tossed aside; I can assure you right now that your copy of <u>The Automated Entrepreneur</u> will become so worn and dog-eared from multiple readings—not to mention filled with notes and highlighted passages—that you'll want to buy another copy just to have a new, clean, unmarked version to lend your colleagues and friends. (After all, sharing business strategies is one thing, but you're not about to lend your own treasure trove of insights that you stumbled upon while reading this book!)

The all-encompassing combination of strategies within this book will give you the means to create your own ideal lifestyle and live the good life while you watch the success of your business skyrocket beyond your imagination. In this book, five critical elements will guide you to success:

- Element #1: Analyze your business and lifestyle

- Element #2: Maximize what's making you the most money

- Element #3: Bring in ideal customers

- Element #4: Make money with upsells and cross-sells

- Element #5: Build your dream business

Get your highlighter and favorite pen ready (preferably *after* you've bought this book) because *this starts NOW*. (Okay, I lied; it starts on the next page with the introduction.)

INTRODUCTION

I n late 2009, I was driving home a $100,000 Mercedes truck, brand-spanking-new from the dealership. I was stoked.

"Man, I can't believe how far I've come," I said. That year, my real estate business had brought in around $30 million, and I had everything I ever wanted. But when I parked the Mercedes in the garage an hour later and entered the house, my wife and boy weren't there.

I thought, "Is this it? Is this all I'm working for?" Working 80+ hours a week meant missing the first two years of my son's life, and for what? To buy new things? I hated that lonely, empty feeling I got, and I knew this wasn't what I wanted my life to be.

My parents opened one of the first ethnic grocery stores in my hometown in B.C. From about age 6 to 11, I would help at the store. I loved dealing with people. Hard work was ingrained in me right from the start, along with a love for business.

In high school, my family hit a rough patch. We had experienced losses and break-ins. My parents had no concept of marketing the way we do today. They figured if they could open a retail store, they would make money. The target market was very small and our costs were incredibly high. The funds ran out and we had to close shop.

I did not want to live like that. I love to play soccer, and with three brothers, it was tough to put us in any after-school activities with the costs being so high. We couldn't even afford our soccer league fees: I had to throw a paper route just to play soccer. When I was a kid, I just wanted to get out on the field; soccer was my passion.

Everywhere I went, I felt I had to prove something to somebody. My fear of failure motivated me to excel at any job I could get: selling chocolate bars door-to-door, throwing papers, and telemarketing on the weekends. Money was a major motivator, too. I sold the most chocolate bars and made most of the sales for the telemarketing firm. I loved it. I figured if I had enough money, I could buy whatever I wanted and be happy.

Prior to 2009, I worked three jobs while putting myself through a couple years of college. I got my certification with Microsoft and became an analyst at the Insurance Corporation of British Columbia (I.C.B.C.). When I started work, I saw people who had been there for 30 years who were slouched over their computers, miserable. I remember thinking to myself, "Is this it? Is this what my life is gonna look like?" I said, "There's got to be a better way. I can't keep doing this."

With the money I made from I.C.B.C., I started flipping properties in downtown Vancouver. I would buy a property that wasn't even built yet and flip paper for $2,000, $5,000, or even $10,000. I ended up getting my real estate license, quit my job at I.C.B.C., and did what 95 percent of other real estate agents do: plastered ads with ego-driven pictures of myself on the back of bus benches, newspapers, TV, promoting the traditional "retail" real estate services.

I struggled on the well-tread path for about seven years: $100,000 in, $100,000 out. Needing to find a different way, I started to invest in myself through seminars, programs, mentors, and other tools to fast-track my success. I called that investment "buying speed." Now, people buy "speed" from me, too: the invaluable processes, systems, and shortcuts from my business.

One day, my mentor said something to me: "Why sell one home when you can sell ten homes to the same person?" Nobody wanted to deal with real estate investors because they would low-ball offers and waste time. Our breakthrough was positioning ourselves as the go-to real estate investment brokerage.

I built a system where we trained beginning investors to buy property in their own neighborhoods. In about 21 months, we went from getting $150,000 in my regular business to making around $35 million in sales, even expanding to employ over 20 people. Since then, I look at a business and ask, "What can we do that everybody else is **not** doing?"

Right after I bought my Mercedes in 2009, I realized I was working too hard. When I was growing up, my parents hadn't spent much time with me because they were working to support our family. I didn't want that for my family. I wanted to be a part of my kids' life. I had more than I needed, but I was still working too much. I looked within myself and said, "Where am I going with this? What do I want to do?"

I scaled down the real estate business and hired a personal growth mentor. I needed to learn to channel the energy, fears, and money I had into an ideal lifestyle. I wanted to spend more time with my family. I wanted to be able to pick up my son at 2:30 from school every single day. I wanted to take him to soccer practice, I wanted to coach his team. I couldn't do any of that, so I shifted my business to make time for my family.

I learned to automate many processes in my business and other businesses. I gained knowledge by building that business from the ground up and by studying other successful businesses and their systems. Seeing businesses fail all around me taught me how not to run a business. I had a friend who bought into a franchise and spent over $300,000 to set up a retail store, but only made a couple thousand dollars a month. He and his wife worked over 70 hours a week there. Spending $300,000 to make $2,500 per month is ludicrous. As I started to research more and more, I found this to be true of hundreds of local businesses in my area. That kind of return just didn't make sense to me.

As I started working on myself personally, my business approach shifted to focus on marketing and automation. In my business, we ask about the business owner's ideal lifestyle. Once we know what that is, we create a plan. We look at your current lifestyle and discover how much money you need to make each month, how many hours you want to work, and every other important factor in creating your ideal lifestyle. Then we set up the business processes to help you live that ideal lifestyle. We reverse engineer everything. We automate clients' marketing by creating playbooks, scripts, videos, podcasts, books, and business processes.

Most business owners don't do this; they open up shop and just work. Probably fewer than 5 percent of business owners follow their actual business plan (if they even have one), especially in the small business market—they're too busy working in their business. They have no structure and they end up with many haphazard marketing programs that get them nowhere. I fix all of that and get it running like a well-oiled machine.

Many things can be automated. I use technology and systems to give me time to do what I love while providing a better experience overall. For example, in my real estate business, I was wasting hours on training people. I thought, "Why don't I just build this thing once and let people watch it, and if they have any questions, they can ask me?" So I built the playbook for our business, using this model for every position within our organization.

I used a real "set and forget" approach. Today, I build playbooks for other companies.

I can fast-track anybody's success. I know exactly how to walk into a business and find hundreds of thousands of dollars that can be regained with little or no work.

I started to leverage people right from the beginning. When I was flipping houses, I needed more volume, but didn't want to work so hard. I said, "I'm just going to find myself a student that needs some extra cash to go find me some properties, and I'll pay 'em." So I did. That's what I do today: I leverage people and technology to create my ideal lifestyle.

It's all about your lifestyle. Even today, I sometimes get drawn in where money becomes that motivator or main goal. So I take a step back and look at it: "Is this aligned with what I want in terms of my lifestyle?" That's what we're talking about in this book: using systems and automation to get time for your family while your business flourishes.

Now you know my story. Welcome to *The Automated Entrepreneur: How to Boost Sales, Maximize Profits, & CRUSH the Competition*. This is your ultimate playbook to working less, making more, and creating your ideal stress-free lifestyle. While some so-called experts encourage people to rely solely on S.E.O., referrals, or direct mail marketing to build their customer base, the truth is that if you want your business to skyrocket, a multi-channel approach is an absolute must.

Within the pages of this book, you will learn the secrets to enhancing your business for optimal profits and stability. Many business owners have just one question in the beginning: "How can I grow my business?" The key to growing your business is found in the second critical element of this book, "Maximize What Makes the Most Money," which details how to begin attracting only your ideal clients. Those are the clients who will pay what your product or service is really worth—which increases your revenue, cuts your workload, and frees your time so you can spend it on other things.

That's only a small preview of what's awaiting you in this gold mine of innovative strategies, which teaches you how to overcome the most common obstacles that would-be successful business owners encounter—and how to shift your focus to what's most important. Part of that shift requires making the best possible use of your time while at work; check out page #101 to find out exactly why it is vital to only ever work at your highest revenue-creating capacity (and how you can still get less lucrative tasks done), which action #89, #90, and #91 detail in the fifth critical element.

Eventually, we all ask ourselves, "Is my business supporting my ideal lifestyle?" Your business needs to support you, not the other way around. The knowledge and tools that you will receive in these pages will enable you to envision—and then create— your dream lifestyle. Make your dream lifestyle a reality by systemizing, optimizing, and monetizing your business—on autopilot!

Maybe I should let you discover this on your own when you reach the fifth critical element of this book, but I cannot emphasize this enough: start working on your business, not in it, if you want to begin living your ideal lifestyle. Can't wait to get to that final chapter? Flip through to page #98 and read action #85 ("Work on Your Business, Not in It") before you return to this introduction.

In this book, you will learn how to crush the competition and become the leader in your industry, exponentially increase your referrals, cut your staffing costs by one-third, automate virtually everything in your business, and much more. Honestly, you can't afford to skip this. You will even learn how to build your very own virtual marketing department that costs less than a part-time employee!

This book will not just help you to create your dream business. It will give you the steps to completely overhaul it, bringing you an abundance of ideal clients that return more often and spend more money every time.

Still don't know if you should put down the $19.97 for this book? Let's be real, here: you've just selected the one business book that will not only easily save you thousands, but will also cut your workload in half and double your sales. It's worth its weight in gold. Now that's a smart investment!

Throughout this book, we will be using a simple format to address each of the questions and concerns you will have about becoming an "automated" entrepreneur with the stress-free freedom to live your ideal lifestyle. In this book, we have simplified the process with five critical elements to guide you in your entrepreneurship journey; in each element, there are questions and supporting actions (numbered for your convenience) that will help you boost sales, maximize profits, and CRUSH the competition. Get ready to systemize, optimize, and monetize your business on autopilot!

Get instant access to over $693.31
of pure money-making strategies.

Plus, get a 30-minute strategy session (a $497 value)
absolutely FREE.

Register now at www.BobMangat.com/Book-Offer.

ELEMENT #1:
ANALYZE YOUR BUSINESS
& LIFESTYLE

"The beginning is the most important part of the work."
—Plato

In this first chapter, we will be focusing on analyzing your company's cash flow and marketing efforts. We will not only be looking at how much money your business is bringing in every month, but also at where you're making the most money, how you can start working for your best clients, and how becoming a qualified expert in your niche increases the quality of your offering and your bottom line.

You can think of this stage as the health assessment of your business by analyzing your current financial situation. Know where you're at before you begin working towards changing your business—and, ultimately, creating your ideal lifestyle. This first critical element to building a successful business and ideal lifestyle guides you through the following five questions:

- Question #1: How much money do you make, and where do you make the most money?

- Question #2: Where is your money coming from?

- Question #3: What is your marketing strategy for ensuring cash flow?

- Question #4: How are your marketing efforts really working?

- Question #5: How do people support your marketing efforts?

Grab a notebook and pen to take notes; you're going to extract tons of useful information throughout this chapter and the rest of the book.

Ready? Great! Read on to start learning how to market your ideal products and services in a way that appeals to your top clients.

Question #1:
How Much Money Do You Make, & Where Do You Make the Most Money?

Action #1: Evaluate Your Income

When I am working with a business owner, the first thing I want to know is how much they make. I don't want to know anything else at that point. I'm surprised by the number of businesses I deal with on a daily basis that don't know what they actually make.

You need to know these numbers. If you don't already immediately know how much you make, take the time to figure out how much revenue your business is earning before you continue reading.

Action #2:
Determine How Much Money You Want to Make

Often, business owners with whom I work notice a gap between how much money they're making and how much they want to make. When things aren't happening, it's their responsibility to find out why they're not earning what they want to earn.

There are so many reasons why somebody might not be earning what they want to earn. They could have be working too much in their business and not working on it. It could be a staffing issue, or a lack of knowledge about marketing or advertising. Maybe they've had some family or health issues that stunted their business growth, or had problems acquiring enough capital to get their business off the ground.

Likewise, you might have several reasons why you're not making what you should make. Maybe you just got into the business because you love what you do. Unfortunately, passion is just not enough these days to guarantee success.

In the next action step, we will be looking at what you can do to close the gap between how much money you're making and how much you want to make.

Action #3: Calculate Your Current Net Profit

In the businesses that I look at, net profit can fluctuate substantially. After I find out how much a business owner is making and wants to make, I ask, "How much goes in your bank account at the end of the month?"

Many businesses are focused on a month-to-month basis; they're basically strapped for cash—especially smaller businesses. When you can't forecast what your business revenues will be, you can't accurately forecast what your expenses should be or what you will take home. It's a rat race you'll never win. We want to be able to create consistent, predictable, reliable income month after month, year after year.

When I ask about net profit, what I'm really asking is, "How much money do you keep?" From there, we can start to figure out what the next steps will be.

Action #4: Set a Goal for Your Net Profit

Often, if I go through the questions discussed in the first three action steps with a business owner, I find that they don't know where they're going or why they're doing what they're doing. Similarly, maybe you got into business because you love what you do, but you're not building any real equity; you're not building a real, potentially saleable, business.

Visualize what your ideal lifestyle would look like. Be specific about what it is that you want. If you want a car, visualize the make, model, color, and any custom add-ons you want. If you want a vacation, visualize the location, activities, number of people accompanying you, and the weather. Maybe you want to go to the Bahamas with your wife and two kids, spending time on the beach on a sunny day. Whatever it is, be specific when you imagine what you want.

Next, I want you to figure out how much these things will cost. Once you have a good estimate, you can then work backwards and determine how much money you want or need to make. (Read more about this in action #16.)

Many people aren't looking at marketing as something that they like doing; they got into their industry because that's what they do. But once you start seeing marketing as what makes your desired lifestyle possible, that motivates you to start researching and learning how to excel at marketing your business.

It's not about the service you offer so much so in the beginning, as much as people would like to think of it as that. Don't get me wrong; the service aspect of things goes a long way. But customers have to experience the service first, right? Well, if you can't get them in the door, then how can they try what you're offering? You have to get your clients in first. The bulk of your time should be focused on acquiring clients. Eighty percent of your time should be spent on getting new people in, getting people to buy more, or getting people to buy other stuff.

Customer referrals are vital, but sometimes we forget about asking for referrals or we just don't even know about how useful they are. Getting referrals is one of the key aspects to a successful marketing strategy. Most business owners will just take appointments, and by the time the end of the day rolls around, they don't have time to do any marketing. That's the wrong way to grow a business.

If you're in business, you need to put all of your marketing tools into play. If you don't have the time, then find the time. It's a must. This aspect of your business should not be overlooked or left in the hands of anyone else in your organization.

Not getting the right type of new clients is the number one reason why there can be such a big gap between how much you make and how much you want to make. If you don't acquire the right clients who will pay what you're worth, you're wasting your time. In action #5, we'll look at how to start earning more without necessarily putting in additional hours.

Question #2: Where Is Your Money Coming From?

Action #5:
Notice Where You Make the Most Money

Do you have shiny object syndrome? Are you stepping over dollars to pick up pennies? Often, over the years, we start adding different services to our business. Maybe a client tells us, "You know, maybe you should add this to your business. I could come in here and do a one-stop shop type of deal. That would be so much easier." Trying to be everything to everyone is overwhelming and reduces your potential for profit. Without a specialized niche, the skill and attention to detail in your services plummets. You don't get the wealth of experience that comes from focusing on what you do best and what generates the most money.

Maybe you started adding a whole bunch of different products or services to bring in more clients. But once you closely look at the services that you're offering, you might realize you're trying to promote way more than the one thing that brings you the most revenue.

Lacking a strong focus ends up confusing you and detracts from what you actually need to do. More importantly, it confuses your prospects or clients. Very early on in my career, I learned how important it is to stop stepping over dollars to pick up pennies. Find out what brings in the most revenue, and then focus on that.

Look at how much money you make. Where do you make the most money? Exactly which service or product brings in the most revenue? This should give you a sharp, clear picture as to where you should focus more of your time.

For example, if you have a service or product that brings in about 70 or 80 percent of your revenue, but you're only focusing 20 percent of your time on marketing that service or product, there's a problem. If that service or product is what's making you the most money, you should be focusing much more of your time on getting more customers interested in that specific service or product.

Action #6: Determine What You Are Skilled at That Makes You Good Money

Most people know what they are skilled at that makes them good money. Be true to your core business offerings. Focus on making those the best they can be before venturing out and adding other products and services.

This element is about opening your eyes to see what you're good at, why you fell in love with the business in the first place, and what makes you the most amount of money. Don't leave your products or services to chance. Find out what sparks the most interest in your customer base, and go after that.

Action #7: Offer Your Ideal Services That Generate the Most Revenue

With the advent of Groupon, some people are adjusting their businesses because they think that they need to compete on price. In fact, that's the furthest from the truth: there are deal-hunters (and you can let other people who don't understand the concepts in this book have those people), but there are also people who are willing to pay more for better service.

In essence, instead of having thousands of clients, you may have a hundred clients who are paying more for your services. It's easier to sell high-priced products or services to a select few than to sell low-priced products or services to a large pool of customers. That way, you don't have to rely on finding any person who is willing to spend a few bucks before going on to the next guy. These types of low-paying customers are not loyal to your business and will cause you more problems than anything. Stay away from this type of business.

You can keep your high-paying clients longer by offering them greater value, thereby building customer loyalty. I call this the "less clients, more money" strategy.

Look at the services you're offering. Are they making you money? We will go into more detail later on in this book, but for now, consider whether the services that you're offering are making you enough money. If they're not making enough money, improve them or cut them out of your business.

Action #8: Your Effort-Profit Ratio: Assess the Profitability of Your Service or Product

The effort-profit ratio is a very simple question: "If it's not making you money, then why are you doing it?" Too many people put in the right effort but do so in the wrong areas. They put in all the right amount of work in terms of promoting a product or a service or an event, but it's not a profitable venture. It may look like a profitable venture from the outside, but it isn't: there's little or no profit. Look at your services and figure out what's profitable and what's not. That assessment will show you where to spend the most effort.

Most of the time, people will tell me the services where there's little effort and good profit. That makes it easy to get them started generating a lot of money. Once you find those high-profit areas, you need to figure out how to get those ideal clients in the door.

When you ask yourself, "Are my services making me money?" you have to look at your pricing. Often, people say, "I need to undercut the competition to compete or be in line with market rates." However, I have a different philosophy on that: I tell business owners, "Raise your prices 20 to 30 percent, and you'll outcompete." The high-paying customers in your target market will look at that and say, "Man, I wonder what they provide for that extra 30 percent." Essentially, the key is to provide more value than your competitors. That extra 30 percent should not be an arbitrary price hike, but should account for the greater value that you provide.

Question #3: What Is Your Marketing Strategy for Ensuring Cash Flow?

Action #9: Market Your Business Online

If you're not making use of online marketing, you're destined for failure. Take some time to construct a clear, detailed strategy for promoting your products or services to your ideal prospects. Write it down and don't be afraid to revise your plan as you learn what works and what doesn't. Testing and tracking campaigns is key to winning in online business.

When I ask about online marketing, most of the time, business owners say, "Oh, I have a website, and I post on Facebook once or twice a week." Sadly, a website or a couple of social media posts isn't good enough to create substantial results. You need to actively promote it, or else you'll never get enough traffic to your site.

You need to create a cohesive online presence that works for your particular niche. Get your "social focus" going: promote your business on Twitter, Snapchat, Instagram, Facebook, Pinterest, Periscope, and/or other relevant social media sites. Depending on your niche, products, and services, you may find one or more of these social channels more useful than the rest (or even decide that some are not the ideal tool for connecting to your audience).

Part of your social focus is finding out where your target market is. If you're a business-to-business company, then you should be on LinkedIn or similar sites and use most of your social media marketing time there.

Once you know where your customers are hanging out, research what approaches from the competition work and what don't. Don't just look at them and say, "Hey, that ad they're running is nice." Dive deep into the competitor research and figure it out. For example, some Facebook users may feel uncomfortable with businesses that approach them directly; to the business owner, they may be simply anticipating customer needs, but to the potential customer, it may be seen as an invasion of privacy.

Another issue is sincerity: sometimes, business accounts on Facebook appear to be insincere or "trying too hard," which compromises trust and effective branding. Learn how to connect with social media users without overstepping the bounds or being written off as insincere—all by seeing where your competition has misstepped.

Keeping your local listings updated is also important. Make sure your business name, category, address, phone, images, and other details are correctly listed in places where people may be searching for your products or services. YellowPages, Google Maps, Yahoo!, Yelp, and other directories are just some of the places where your customers are hanging out. You can also get great reviews from your customers posted on those directory sites, which increases your credibility and also helps with your search rankings.

Directory listing managers, such as ExpressUpdate.com or Yext.com, are a quick way to spot errors and fix them without spending half of the day going from site to site. My company, invigoMEDIA.com, also provides a free 12-page report on how to manage your local listings and web presence; the report shows all of this and more.

Action #10: Use Offline Marketing Strategies

Offline strategies include direct mail, cold-calling, newspaper advertising, and customer service calls to engage customers again, to name a few. These old school techniques, when combined with online marketing, can have a great impact on your bottom line. If you integrate your offline strategies with your online strategies, it can significantly boost your referrals and new client generation.

If you only have one offline marketing strategy, then you will have limited results that are confined to that specific strategy. By itself, cold calling may get you a few clients. Referrals may get you a few clients, direct mail may get you a few, and so forth. To grow your business, you should use multiple channels to bring in your ideal clients.

I call this creating pillars in your business. Imagine a home standing on one pillar: if that single pillar breaks, that home is going to come crashing down. Now think of a house that has six or eight pillars. If one breaks, the others will carry the load, allowing you time to fix the one that is broken without seeing any significant decrease in support (revenue). This is especially important in uncertain economic times. Businesses go out of business because they don't have additional pillars (marketing strategies) to rely on. Don't be like 95 percent of other businesses out there. Learn this stuff and it will make your business that much stronger.

Most business owners call their local newspaper and say, "I'd like to run an ad." They then think that just because it's the main newspaper in their market, they'll get some good distribution and readers will see it. After all, that newspaper has hundreds of thousands of readers. But how do you know you're reaching the people with whom you want to do business? If you're a chiropractor, do you know how many people who that read that newspaper actually have back pain?

Don't sell yourself short by relying on a single strategy that may be ineffective. Be strategic about where you spend your money. Just because your competitor is advertising in that paper doesn't mean you have to advertise there, too. Research whether the people who will see (and, hopefully, read) your advertisement include a pool of potentially interested customers. Most businesses rely on a single method to generate business and don't plan their campaign carefully. That gives you an instant advantage if you diversify your campaign to include multiple outlets.

You need to find out how to reach the right people with your campaigns. A newspaper ad won't work if your target market doesn't subscribe to the paper. Sending postcards won't work if your target market routinely ignores unsolicited mail, or if you send the postcards to people who aren't part of your target market. Don't limit yourself to a single strategy. Create a web of strategies that include at least five or six different methods of acquiring leads and generating new business.

Action #11: Use Inbound Marketing to Your Advantage

"Inbound marketing refers to marketing activities that bring visitors in, rather than marketers having to go out to get prospects' attention. Inbound marketing earns the attention of customers, makes the company easy to be found, and draws customers to the website by producing interesting content."
(Source: Wikipedia.)

Are you creating educational content for your prospects and distributing it on social sites such as Facebook, Twitter, or YouTube? Don't act too salesy here. Create educational-based content that builds expert status in the eyes of your prospects.

Consider your specific process of handling clients. What is your intake process? Do you have a process in place for acquiring testimonials? If you don't already have a system for your inbound marketing efforts, now is the time to create one. Write scripts for your staff so that they are prepared when someone calls or visits your business. Keep track of how many people call versus visiting, along with any other relevant details, including your conversion rate.

Hold regular staff meetings in which you exchange ideas and ensure that your staff meets or exceeds your clients' needs. (Bonus: asking for input from your employees, particularly when you use their suggestions, boosts employee morale and loyalty, as they feel more involved in the business even by contributing a single idea or suggestion.) Encourage your staff to convert more prospects into clients, and always give your staff time to ask you any questions that they may have.

Action #12: Outbound Marketing: Contact Your Customers Regularly

Keeping in contact with your customers is vital, particularly for businesses that rely on repeat customers. It is much more time- and cost-effective to keep getting business from the same customers than to focus on continually acquiring new one-time customers.

Write down your current strategy and look for any gaps. For example, are you sending email reminders to all of your clients, despite the fact that some of them are elderly and are more likely to prefer a good old-fashioned phone call? How often do you follow up with customers? What is their usual response, and how can you encourage them to continue doing business with you?

Evaluate your telemarketing, sales, or outbound calling strategy. Who are you calling? Are you just picking up the phone and calling anybody? If you are scrambling to get business—such as if you own a clinic that hasn't had patients come in for a while— target your efforts on those who are most likely to need your services again. It's easier to sell to an established client than to sell to someone completely new.

Using more than one point of contact will give you better results. You could couple your offline strategies with mailing postcards to a specific local demographic and then follow up with a phone call to each postcard recipient. Not only will you be getting that person's attention with an offline postcard and (through compelling ad copy) driving them to your website, but you will also be calling them to ask whether they received your information and would like to schedule an appointment. Consider including a direct response special offer with a time or limit scarcity in your postcard, such as, "Get a free 15-minute consultation (a $497 value), yours free if you respond within 5 days." This is a direct offer that will have them responding to something of value. If you don't already have a strategy in place, create a specific process and adjust it as you learn what does and doesn't work.

Question #4: How Are Your Marketing Efforts Really Working?

Action #13: Duplicate Your Business' Best Year

When people are in business for a certain amount of time, they will say, "Back in this day, we used to make X amount."

I have a client who told me recently, "Bob, I've been around for thirty years, and my business has been ever-declining since."

And I said, "Well, it's because you haven't embraced change. Change is happening all around you. You think that just because you've been around for thirty years that people will just come to you. And that's not the case."

Sure, you have past customers that trust you and will always do business with you. But what about new customers? If you're not investing in your digital presence, embracing change, and being where your customers are looking for you, then your sales will decline, eventually putting you out of business.

The first couple of years, a business typically does quite well; that's because new business owners watch every penny; they are very careful where they spend. It's usually around the third or fourth year that they start to struggle as they tend to shift their focus away from their clients' needs and focus on their own instead, especially in their marketing campaigns.

Rather than believing, "We *have* to get new clients or we'll sink," businesses that have been around for years are usually less customer-oriented and may have lost or weakened their connection with their clients. You can see this in the difference between the business' advertising or marketing as they were starting to grow, and the advertising or marketing later on.

In the beginning, most people rely on raw marketing materials that are precise, to the point, and not so flashy. But once they start making some money, they hire a designer and start to professionally brand their products or services. They don't understand why, but their results start to dip.

It's because their messaging and their focus is no longer geared towards getting people in; they're trying more to promote themselves than to show the customer, "Here's what's in it for you." If you focus on creating your message with the "What's in it for me?" attitude, you will get much better results than by focusing on flashy brand-based ads.

Action #14: Compare What's Working Now with What Worked in the Past

What we need to find out is when the best year was for your business. Look back at that year. What was your marketing strategy like?

Get back into the mindset that you had when your business was doing well. You might go over your marketing materials, notes, and any other pertinent data to help you to recreate what worked in the past. By repeating the same strategies that you used in the best year of your business, you can recreate that scenario in which you had plenty of revenue and your business was successful.

Action #15: Focus on Revenue-Generating Activities

Many of us begin our workday by checking our email, paying some bills, or doing some paperwork. Everybody's got to do that, but from there, we may become distracted with tasks that are less important than what we should be spending our time on.

Instead, you should focus on what will bring you revenue today. What is the best use of your valuable time? Is it picking up the phone and calling some of your best clients, referral sources, or partners? Are you doing those things that will bring you revenue in the immediate future, or are you squandering your time doing something menial, such as cleaning the office or trying to fix a piece of equipment?

Every day, you should focus on revenue-generating activities, not doing the tasks of a janitor. For your business to grow, you can't use your time doing things that you could hire someone to do for $10, $15, or $20 an hour. Hire someone else to be your janitor; you have more lucrative things to do today (and every day). Spend your time using the skills you have that bring in the most revenue.

I had coffee with a friend the other day, and he told me, "So, I've got this five-year plan."

I said, "Well, that's great; what's your plan for tomorrow?"

He said, "Oh, I'm going to go to the beach. I'm going to hang out."

I said, "Okay, that's great. You're not going to get to that five-year plan if you're going to do that."

In order to meet your five-year plan, you need to focus on

your daily goals rather than your one-year, two-year, or five-year goals. If you do what you need to do today to generate business, then your five-year plan will fall in line.

Action #16: What Are You Doing Daily to Achieve Your Lifestyle Goal?

I started to do five-year plans, but I don't do them anymore. Instead, I rely on daily plans. If I do whatever I need to do on a daily basis, I will achieve my goals for the year.

You don't have to create a five-year plan, but you do need to know what you're going to be doing every day to work towards your goals. You could plan to make $100,000 in the next month or two, buy a house, or take your family on vacation. Whatever your goal is, write it down and then simplify it to create your daily plan to achieve that goal.

Break it down and reverse engineer the whole process. For example, let's say you need to buy a new car. Most people will check the balance in their savings account, go to the dealership, and then purchase the vehicle. I'm the complete opposite. I say, "How many clients do I need to get so I can buy that new car without changing my lifestyle?"

When you do the math, that car might cost you $1,000 a month over a span of X number of years. Jot down how many clients you need per month to pay that $1,000 car payment in addition to your regular bills.

Try to improve your financial position before taking on additional debt. Find out what you have to do on a daily basis to achieve your goals, whether that's purchasing a vehicle or putting your kids through college.

I look at financial goals from a day-to-day perspective, but I also keep a bird's-eye view of what I'm doing. I wait until I have enough clients to buy that home or car that we want, and have that freedom to keep our lifestyle the same. We still take the same number of vacations and stay at 5-star resorts. We still save the same amount of money for our kids' education and activities. I can still wear nice clothes, I can still go to 5-star restaurants, I can still entertain. I can still do all those things without adding stress and affecting my daily life.

Look at the payoff that you'll get from making those investments, whether it's an investment of time, a lifestyle adjustment, or anything else. Imagining what the end result will be can motivate you, just as marking your progress by keeping a daily journal of what you did that day to reach your goals can.

Question #5: How Do People Support Your Marketing Efforts?

Action #17: Manage Your Marketing Efforts

Whether you're working for yourself or have a big business with 30 employees, you need to create and use a strategic marketing plan. Decide whether you will manage all of your marketing ad campaigns or whether you will hire outside talent to handle those things.

If you've already done that, it's time to review what you've got so far. Take a look at your inbound and outbound strategies. What are you doing online? What are you doing offline? Who is handling all of those activities, and are they all in sync? Does the rest of the staff know what you're promoting? Do they know your marketing plan?

Make sure that your team is communicating with one another about what they're doing. If you're running it all by yourself, check at least on a weekly basis that your marketing strategies are fulfilling your needs and expectations.

Action #18: Ensure That You Have the Expertise Necessary to Attract Business

Just because you think you know a few things about running an advertisement doesn't mean that you can necessarily produce good results on a consistent basis. Having expertise on your side (or being an expert yourself) is an absolute must. You need to either learn it—and with all of the digital changes that are happening right now, that can be quite challenging—or get someone else to handle that. I attribute much of my success to my mentors and the mastermind groups I belong to that help me take shortcuts and fast-track my success.

Put people in the places where you're not the most effective. If you've been to school for eight years and you become an M.D., chances are you haven't learned much about marketing. You were learning about saving lives, and that's what you have to continuously do: save lives.

This goes back to the idea of spending your time wisely. If you're not very effective at creating marketing materials, you can hire a freelancer or company to do that. Instead of squandering dozens or even hundreds of hours trying to learn how to use PhotoShop, write good ad copy, and use consumer psychology to create an effective campaign, you could hire someone who does nothing but create ad campaigns—and then spend those saved hours on activities that will further boost your revenue.

It's likely that you can't afford *not* to hire an assistant. All of those hours that you would have spent trying to learn something you don't have the knack for can be used more effectively elsewhere, saving you money and the frustration of seeking to form a new skill set from nothing.

Action #19: Regularly Track Your Marketing Efforts

When I speak with business owners, I ask them, "How do

you track your marketing efforts?" Often, they say, "Well, when people come in, we ask, 'Where did you hear about us?'" That's not trackable. You want to know the exact source that brought them to your business. Which advertisement, magazine issue, newspaper, or website was it? Did a search on Google, Yahoo!, or Bing attract their interest? Was it Facebook, LinkedIn, a postcard, or a referral? Keep a spreadsheet of these items, and then log how much money each customer spent on your products or services.

What we want to find out is where the most profitable customers are and how much it costs to acquire each of those customers. You should start to use Google Analytics and a customer relationship management (C.R.M.) system. Those tools will tell you exactly how that person found your business, what it took to get them to go through your doors, and how much you spent to reach that person. My business uses Infusionsoft for our C.R.M., but there are other less expensive alternatives available if you're just starting.

Consider relying more on whichever method has been bringing in your best clients. Is there a specific advertising medium that appeals to them, or a specific area where many of your clients live? When you track your customer metrics, you should look at not just where your clients come from, but also how much you spent to get that client, and how much they spent over the next 12, 24, or 36 months. You also want to track the number of referrals that person sent you. When you have that, you'll have an average customer value. This will give you a good idea on what to spend to acquire a new customer, and should formulate the basis of your customer acquisition strategy.

Knowing the value of your customers influences the way you treat them. Download your free Lifetime Value Profit (LVP) calculator at www.BobMangat.com/LVP.

Action #20: Keep Your Team Accountable for Achieving Target Goals

You may have different ways to track or incentivize your team to keep them accountable for reaching specific target goals. Do you have target goals? Are there sales goals or other metrics that you're using?

Sometimes, it might not be a sales target that you're looking at. You can also measure things such as how many online reviews you're getting in a week or a month. How many referrals did you get this month? How many new consultations did you book this week or month? What's your conversion rate? Did your conversion rate go from 10 percent to 20 percent?

Achieving these target goals has a direct effect on your brand, overall reputation, and client acquisition. Keep the motivation going by providing incentives for people. You could run contests within your organization to motivate your team. Use a system where you're keeping people accountable for hitting targets. That's critical if you want to get the lifestyle that you're shooting for.

Element #1 Conclusion

In this book's first critical element, we have looked at your current income, which service or product brings you the most revenue, and how tracking your efforts works. Hopefully, you took the time to set a daily goal for increasing the revenue that your business generates. If not, take a moment to figure out how much you need to make. Account for your current and anticipated expenses, debts (if any), desired take-home pay, and remember to add in a little extra as a financial buffer.

Within this chapter, we also discovered whether your current marketing strategies are giving you the results you need, as well as how you can keep your team motivated to consistently meet the target goals that you set. Read on to discover in the second critical element of this book how you can maximize your profits.

ELEMENT #2: MAXIMIZE WHAT MAKES THE MOST MONEY

"If you can't state your position in eight words, you don't have a position."
—Seth Godin

In this second chapter, we will be focusing on detailing exactly who your ideal client is and how you can draw them to your business. Find out how to get inside the mind of those ideal customers and figure out exactly what kind of solution would work best for them. Set yourself apart from the competition by choosing a specific niche and promoting the products and services that will grab the attention of your ideal client. Within this chapter, you will also discover how you can use the competition to your advantage when working on improving your business.

This second critical element to building a successful business and ideal lifestyle guides you through the following five questions:

- Question #6: Who is your ideal client—what is your niche?

- Question #7: What would your perfect customer look like?

- Question #8: What is the pain that your ideal or perfect customer has?

- Question #9: Where are your clients looking for solutions?

- Question #10: How do you make your business stand out in your target market?

Read on to start learning how to grow your business by attracting more of your ideal clients and offering high-quality solutions that meet the needs of a specific niche.

Question #6: Who Is Your Ideal Client—What Is Your Niche?

Action #21: Identify Who Brings in the Most Money to Your Business

To identify who brings in the most money to a business, I usually ask the business owner to profile the 15 to 20 percent of their client list that makes them the most money. The people in that top 15 to 20 percent of the client list make up the target audience. We want to find out the exact attributes of these people so we can have them in mind when creating, revising, or marketing a product or service. Write down who brings the business the most money, what types of people they are, how they found the business, where they live, what they spend with you on average, and any other relevant data.

You have some customers who bring in a lot of money, and other customers who bring in very little, and you're probably spending the same amount of time and effort on both of them. Often, people who aren't in sales or used to dealing with high-value clients establish their business based on providing services for lower-value clients. That's because they're competing based on price. They tend to do a lot more work with lower-value clients, who can even be more demanding than clients who bring in a lot more revenue.

Once you assess which clients are most valuable to your business, you will be ready to shift your focus to clients that bring the most money and are the least demanding. You don't want to be stuck with a client who barely pays you an acceptable rate, yet expects the world from you. By focusing on the top 15 to 20 percent of your clients, you will get paid what you deserve and get appreciation, not complaints.

Action #22: Specialize (Target a Niche)

Choose clients who are easier to deal with and pay you more. You can work with fewer clients and make more money, which also reduces your customer service and acquisition costs. Basically, you will be attracting higher-paying clients who will spend less time with you and see the value in what you provide. Your hourly rate or R.O.I. will be much greater if you focus on a specific target market, niche, or speciality rather than trying to be something to everyone. You want to get those people in action #21 who will bring you the most money, and then deeply analyze their issues and what you want to specialize in before promoting your niche. Then, be a pro at what you provide your clients, because that will yield much more money and require less time.

Action #23: Drop Your Problem Clients

Problem clients are low-profit, high-maintenance clients. After figuring out which clients bring you the most money, it becomes painful to spend your valuable time with demanding people who are not paying you much. That lends to possibly firing some clients.

Often, business owners don't analyze this. This is perhaps *the* most important part of readying your business for future growth. Finding out where you're making the most money (whether it's a specific service or product) and which clients are bringing you the most money is vital to the success of your company.

The top tier of your clients will bring you much more money and spend much less time with you. They will also be more likely to give you excellent reviews and refer people in their network to you. By firing your problem clients, you will have more time to focus on acquiring more of the clients who bring you the most revenue and give you the most appreciation.

Action #24: Build Your Business around Your Ideal Client

Build your entire business around that top tier of clients who make you a whole lot more money. What we want to do is start to make that shift, and see that building your business around your ideal client can be a big change that will make an incredible difference. The important thing is to start moving away from volume and quantity towards providing quality and high-dollar value for clients who are willing to invest more in your products and services.

Question #7: What Would Your Perfect Customer Look Like?

Action #25: Pick Five Ideal Clients & Describe Their Lives

Pick your five ideal clients and describe their lives. What are their likes and dislikes? What are they into? Consider the fine details when describing their lives, even if you have to interview them or research them on the web. Put yourself in your clients' shoes and see what they really want and need.

Get that information, and then you'll see a common thread among all five of them. Maybe they differ in their likes and dislikes, but there is still a common thread, especially from an income standpoint. For one, your ideal clients have more disposable income. Find out who your ideal clients are. Describe their lives in detail.

Pick the top 20 percent of your business and survey them. There are free survey tools such as SurveyMonkey that you can use to create client surveys with specific questions. Often, we get emails and we don't want to respond, but if you incentivize them or create a contest to complete that, your results will be much better. Do not skip this step. It's important to know who your market is.

Collecting information through surveys or interviews is worth it, since you can get good information on creating the perfect business. We don't want to skimp on this action; don't just bring someone in and say, "Hey, why did you come to us?" or "What do you like to do on the weekends?" You need to have specific data so you can analyze it. A survey is the best way to do that.

Action #26: Build the Persona of Your Perfect Customer

Here, we're talking about psychographics: preferences, such as where they like to shop or eat or what they like to look at online. You want to know their birth date or age, gender, and location. Where do they live? If you're in a blue-collar area, are your clients in the upper-class area? Look at what your clients do on the weekends or on vacations, and look at their user behaviors or digital footprint—do they use Facebook, LinkedIn, or some other social media site?

Much of this research can be done yourself. When you get your surveys back, Google your clients and look at their LinkedIn, Facebook, or Twitter profiles. See what they like and what they dislike, what they're doing on the weekends, and what sparks their interest.

Print out profiles of people and carefully analyze the details of that perfect customer. Get into the specific details; for example, do they use an iPhone? Do they still have a flip phone? That tells you where they are from a technology standpoint. We automatically assume everybody's online and they're on Facebook. Don't assume. While some areas may be highly concentrated with online and mobile activity, many other areas have little online business happening.

Looking at your clients' behaviors from a digital footprint side of things is important. That can be easily done; if you see that your five ideal clients are active Facebook or LinkedIn users, chances are, they're going to be using a mobile phone or smartphone. But if they're not or if they're not very active users, then that's something you want to consider as well; there might be a better way to reach those customers.

Action #27: Define the Demographics of Your Target Group of Customers

Figure out not only who has a need for your product or service, but also who is most likely to buy it. Think about the following factors: age, gender, location, income level, education level, marital status, occupation, and ethnic background. Now, we're beginning to paint a picture of our ideal client.

Action #28: Compare Your Current Customers to This Avatar

Go to Google and get an image of your ideal client. Once you've analyzed their location, age, gender, whether they have kids, what they drive, and other attributes, you can go to Google Images and find a representative picture of that person. If it's a blue-collar worker, you might find someone wearing a hardhat. Save that image when you're doing your profile of that type of person. Doing so gives you a great visual to look at your ideal client in a less abstract way.

Look at how your current customers compare to this avatar. Compare the avatar of this ideal client with the five people who are your best clients or the 20 percent of your client base that you've chosen. Go into more detail. Having done that comparison exercise, you may realize, "If I really want this to work, I'm going to have to change a few things around here."

My question to you is, "Well, why are you dealing with that other percentage of your clients? This is your perfect customer; these are the people who you want to deal with and who will pay you handsomely to provide services."

You can use this ideal customer profile not only for marketing purposes, but also for staffing purposes. You can tell future employees, "This is our perfect client." The person you're trying to hire might not have a good relationship with your ideal client; you want to know that before making a hiring decision. The potential new employee may not be confident dealing with higher dollar value clients.

Asking a student who makes $10 an hour to sell a $10,000 package is, in most cases, a tough task. That may leave you judging job candidates based solely on experience. Don't fall for that trap. They should be adept at cultivating relationships as well.

Most businesses are in a relationship-building business, and I've seen so many times where people will hire the wrong person: someone who doesn't know how to build relationships. That can be a major conversion killer. As one of my early mentors told me, "Fire fast, and hire slow."

Question #8: What Is the Pain That Your Ideal or Perfect Customer Has?

Action #29: Look at What Problem You Think You're Solving

Once you've analyzed who your ideal customers are, you want to analyze the reasons they came in to see you. What issues did they have? They may have seen you from an ad. They may have thought they needed something completely different about your business, but once you brought them in, they had different issues that you needed to tackle.

You'll start to see a recurring theme with your ideal customers or, if you own a clinic, your ideal patients. In my business, I often get people saying, "Well, I just need more customers." They think that's the panacea to building an everlasting business, but sometimes, that's far from the truth. Thriving as a business also has to do with many of the things on the back end. Although a customer might think they need something on the front end, it can go way deeper than that.

Finding out why your customers responded to ads is only part of discovering exactly why your customers are seeking your service. As business owners, we may think that we're providing a service, but oftentimes, the service that the customer gets from us is different than what we had expected.

Action #30: See How This Problem Could Be Impacting Your Clients' Life

Find out exactly why your clients are coming in and what problem you can solve for them. I went to my chiropractor because I wanted to continue to play soccer at a high level. I've been playing the sport since the age of 5, and now my kids are playing soccer, too. I want to be able to show them that Dad can still compete at a high level. I'm not the same guy as I was in my twenties, and I get a few more aches and pains in the morning after I play.

My chiropractor knew exactly what I wanted, and did a great job in understanding the real reason I went to see him. He took the time to understand my needs and what I wanted, and then he created a plan for me to tackle those needs and wants.

Since going to my chiropractor, my game has been on fire. He's delivered on what he said he would do. Now, he could upsell me on anything—I would trust what he says and buy it.

I'm not a complainer, I have some money to spend on this stuff, and I don't cause problems. My chiropractor gave me an 8-month plan, and I bought into it. Progress didn't happen overnight. I committed to the plan and got my desired results with his help.

You see, I'm his ideal client. Most complainers will say, "Yeah, I will do this," but then don't follow through with the actual plan. Whether it's related to their work or their health, they give up.

They don't go through with what they are supposed to do, and they blame others for their mistakes or lack of results. I always say that I am 100 percent responsible for my results. That's the kind of client you want: someone who will commit to their share of the work.

In your business, look at how your clients' lives are being affected. When I visited my previous chiropractor, he did an assessment and then said, "Okay, this is what we need to do. We need to align this and adjust that." I didn't care about the technical side of it; I just wanted to play longer. That's all I wanted, and had he presented it that way, promoting the longevity of the game that I could play, I probably would have kept him.

In my business, I don't change a thing. At the end of the day, it's about the processes that people build in their business and how well they're using them. It doesn't matter whether you're a furniture manufacturer, a real estate company, or a chiropractor: I just position my messaging differently to each target market, because they have different problems.

When I'm marketing to these people, there are specific messages I use to that target market, and that goes for any business. Look at how this problem could be impacting your client's life and approach them from that viewpoint. When you know what's important to them, they'll be willing to pay you double or triple.

Action #31: Offer Additional Solutions to Solve Your Clients' Problems

Choose your positioning statements (your statements of value or unique selling proposition) carefully. In this action step, you will gather all of the information needed to build those statements. You want to find out what other problems your clients are experiencing as a result of their main problem.

I was seeing my chiropractor because I can't run around after my kids for that long. I want to be able to enjoy my time on the field with them. I want my kids to see their dad play and compete at a high level, and to see that he's never given up and is always continuously moving forward. Those were the underlying reasons for me going to a chiropractor. It was more about an emotional connection than anything that I wanted.

So if you connect emotionally with clients, it doesn't matter what you charge; they'll always fall in line, because none of your competitors will connect from an emotional point of view. Emotion makes all the difference in setting yourself apart in a listing of services. When you have that emotion there, you stand out.

What do you do when you first open a business? You go to your competitors and look at their website, marketing materials, and those types of things. Maybe you notice, "I really like what that guy's doing. I'm going to add a piece of what he's doing into my own marketing material. And then I'm going to add a piece of that other guy's because I really like what he's doing. His logo is really nice, and he's got some really great colors."

Industries have evolved over time in this manner. Any industry that you look at has the same thing repeated from one company to another in slightly different ways. It's the one or two businesses that change or defy industry norms that make the world of difference.

Action #32: Consider the Cost of Doing Nothing

If you do nothing differently, you will get the same results as what you're currently getting. You can either continuously use the same approach and get the results you've always gotten, or do something completely different and change your results.

Before making any major changes, look at your client's ideal lifestyle. Personally, I can see the cost of not being able to chase after my kids, or having them see their dad compete at a high level, and what happens if I let this problem get worse. I want to live an active lifestyle, and I want to have people around me who can help me to live that lifestyle. The same goes for your clients: they want someone to support them in creating their ideal lifestyle.

The cost of doing nothing differently is huge. For instance, if my chiropractor had not started to get a better understanding of what my issues were or focusing on what I wanted to do, I would be seeking a different provider elsewhere who would understand that.

This action step is about increasing the present or lifetime value of your customers and keeping them around. Forming an emotional connection increases the longevity of clients; ultimately, if you know the cost of doing nothing, and you can spark that in your initial discussion with your clients, you will get a "Yes" more often.

Question #9: Where Are Your Clients Looking for Solutions?

Action #33: Learn What Your Clients Have Tried in the Past That Has Failed

Before you can give clients the best solution to their problems, you need to know where your clients are looking for solutions and what they have tried in the past that has failed. Using that information, you can create your statement of value or positioning statement (see action #31).

For example, when we analyze our competitors, we look at their business, their website, and the people with whom they have worked. Once we know who our ideal clients are, we can find out what they've used as solutions in the past, what they're doing now, and what they may be planning for the future. We can easily tell what they're failing in and how we can help them.

By knowing these things, you can specialize in a particular

niche, which will give you better clarity to move your business forward. Business becomes easier because you're no longer worried about fifty or a hundred different client profiles; you're focusing on meeting the needs of four or five specific client types. Reducing the number of client types that you are working with, along with doing your research on what hasn't worked for them in the past, allows you to focus much better, create emotional connections, and provide a solution that matches their individual needs.

Action #34: Discover Why Your Clients Continue to Seek a Solution

Clients who continue to seek a solution may do so because they haven't found anyone who's emotionally connected with them or who understands their true needs. The demand in the marketplace is still there because they haven't settled on a solution, which gives you the opportunity to provide a better solution than what anyone else can offer.

Action #35: Consider How Your Clients' Life Would Look with the Ideal Outcome

Earlier in this element, we painted a picture of our ideal client. Now it's time to paint a picture of what their ideal life would look like after they go through your process or use your solution. You can find out what the problem is, where the pain is (which you will disperse), what you know, and what your client has done in the past. Then you can imagine how their life will improve after they've gone through your process.

Be specific and precise about what that ideal outcome or solution would be. You can even get an image from Google of Joe Construction Worker being happy doing what he wants to do with his family so you can visualize what this will look like for each of your clients.

Action #36: Look at Clients' True Motivation for Solving This Problem

When you find out what your clients' motivation is, instead of just knowing the problem, you can increase the amount of work you get and charge a lot more. As we discovered in the previous actions, you should focus on understanding the emotional reasons behind why they want to solve their problems.

Question #10:
How Do You Make Your Business Stand Out in Your Target Market?

Action #37: Find Your Competitors & Check Them Out

If I ask a business owner, they almost always already know who their top competitors are. You likely have an idea of who your competitors are and who's doing the most business in your area or online: who has the biggest newspaper ads, the best YellowPages listing, and so on.

We want to make sure that we know what your competitors are doing. Often, they know what they're doing, but don't know the inner workings of their business or why they're doing so much more business than their competitors. The main thing we want to do is an analysis of our competitors, one by one.

Pick three competitors and look at everything that they've got going on. Are they active on social media? Do they have a website, and how good is it? Is their site mobile-optimized?

Print out their website and learn more about what their services are. Are they doing any search marketing? Do they have any direct mail pieces? If so, where are they sending direct mail?

If it's in your area or you find out where they're sending their information, gather their postcards; build a file for each of these competitors. Sometimes you can even pick up the phone and call them, especially if they provide services at home. If it's local, you may want to send somebody in there to find out how they deal with their customers.

Action #38: What Do Your Competitors Do Well? Where Do They Drop the Ball?

Gather as much information as possible on your competitors so that you can find out what they do well and where they are dropping the ball. Once you've got that information, you will start to see holes in their business. You will see where they're excelling and where they're failing.

Create a winning formula that solves all of those problems and issues. I have a lot of competitors in my industry, but there are three main ones. I've analyzed everything about their business. When a customer or a business calls me and says, "I'm thinking about going with X, Y, or Z competitor," I say, "Yeah, no problem. Go ahead. But here are the problems you'll face," and I give them a list of things to ask the other companies.

I take it to the next level and even give them a checklist of things to look for: I go on to mention, "When you're interviewing certain people, have a checklist. And I'm going to give this to you for free. Go out there and see if these people do these things." That allows them to make a better decision, and they'll remember me for having provided them with that useful tool. In their eyes, I've immediately created value.

Action #39: Create Your Award-Winning Formula That Generates the Results Clients Want (Statement of Value)

Once you know what your competitors are doing to solve their clients' problem, you can start to build a winning statement of value (see actions #31 and #33). Gather all of the information that you've collected so far. As you start to put this together, you will see where you are lacking in your own business, where to focus most of your time, and what's lacking in your competitors' businesses. Now you can start to say, "Well, all of these things that people aren't doing becomes what our winning formula is. We'll offer all of these things and gear it towards this specific niche."

Action #40: Make an Irresistible Offer

It's not enough just to create a statement of value (see actions #31, #33, and #39). Now you've got to start working on how you can get people in with very little effort and get people to trust what you're saying. If they have failed in the past to find a solution and they are still seeking one, they're going to be skeptics. So there are certain things that go into an irresistible offer, such as scarcity or reversing the risk so it falls completely on you (such as offering a free sample or free consultation). Providing something so that they can come in and experience your services for little or no cost is a great way to get clients, but just because you offer something for little or no cost doesn't mean that there is no value. You need to communicate that your offer is one of immense value, because if you don't, they will think it's worthless and won't be serious about your offer.

Figure out what that irresistible offer is by doing your research, which we've discussed in this second element. Discover who your competitors are, notice their offers, and create an irresistible offer on a case-by-case basis. Always offer something to someone that shows them what's in it for them. You have very limited time to get somebody's attention, so make sure that you're offering something valuable and useful that they can try out for little or no cost.

Provide greater value than your competitors. Here's an example of a great offer for a weight loss clinic:

Lose up to 10 inches in 10 days! For only $47, you get a detoxifying herbal body wrap, three laser lipo sessions, and a FREE weight-loss consultation. This EXCLUSIVE OFFER ($247 value) is backed by our 100% satisfaction guarantee! (Limited availability.)

Did you see what I did here? We have these components in this offer:

- The "What's in it for me?" statement

- A low-cost service to try out

- An actual dollar figure ($247) that highlights the immense value

- The scarcity of an exclusive offer

- A 100 percent satisfaction guarantee that reverses the risk

- The time urgency created by the limited availability of the offer

This is much more compelling than just saying, "Get a body wrap for $97.00!" Be creative and do your homework before crafting your offers. As always, you have to make sure you deliver what you're offering.

Element #2 Conclusion

This second critical element is just the beginning in terms of targeting a select audience (your ideal clients) by specializing in the solutions that your ideal customers need. The key is to attract only your best clients, who will pay what your product or service is worth—which increases your revenue, cuts your workload, and frees your time to spend it on other things.

You also learned how to tell a story to your customer that brings them from the pain of their problem to the freedom that comes with the solutions that you can offer them. Lastly, we discussed how providing greater value than the competition can solidify your position as a leader in your particular niche. Read on to discover much more about effectively marketing to your prospects and customers, which will generate more profits and improve your standing as an industry expert.

ELEMENT #3: BRING IN YOUR IDEAL CUSTOMERS

"It's not about ideas. It's about making ideas happen."
—Scott Belsky

I n this third chapter, you will learn how to outdo the competition and win over your ideal clients. You want to be able to step back from your business and enjoy the rest of your life. In this element, we will look at how you can not only automate your day-to-day tasks, but also improve your relationships with clients in the meantime. Additionally, we will go over how you can increase your conversion rate, form a better client base, and simplify your processes for efficiency and ease of mind.

High-paying clients are crucial to your business success, and this chapter will go over virtually everything that you need to know about targeting your market, approaching potential customers, drawing them in, and, finally, successfully forming an ideal client base. This third critical element to building a successful business and ideal lifestyle guides you through the following five questions:

- Question #11: How will you find your ideal clients?

- Question #12: How do you get your prospects' attention?

- Question #13: How do you follow up with prospects?

- Question #14: How do you get your clients in the door?

- Question #15: How do you convert prospects into clients?

The messages that you promote through your business are important, but just as important is the mode of communication that you use. In this chapter, you will discover which resources will help you to reach your customers and get them to hear what you're saying.

Keep reading to discover how to use both online and offline marketing strategies to reach out to customers and prospects alike, inviting them to consider the services and products that your business provides.

Question #11:
How Will You Find Your Ideal Clients?

Action #41: Use B2B Resources: Network, LinkedIn, & InfoUSA

"B2B" means business-to-business. If you are in B2B, your customers are other businesses. There are tons of different strategies you can use in B2B marketing. Attend association or trade events where you can network with other business owners or go to your local chamber of commerce.

You may be able to advertise and be a speaker at your chamber of commerce; contact the chairman to ask about pitching your product or services there, especially if you own a local business. *That's their job*: promoting local businesses. If your business is regional or national, you may want to find other avenues for attracting different businesses and forming relationships with the key players within various companies.

Many businesses use Facebook, Instagram, or Twitter to market their services; that strategy works really well from a consumer standpoint. Social media channels can also be great B2B advertising sources. I've found it to be hit-and-miss, because they are generally used as consumer sites and most of the users aren't in "business mode." However, I have had great success with LinkedIn, whose users are in business mode and are more open to connecting. That's the whole purpose of the site: connecting with other professionals and doing business.

You can find basically anything you want about anybody on LinkedIn. If their profiles are active, you can find C.E.O.s of major Fortune 500 companies and see who their connections are. You can send them direct messages and try to establish a relationship or connection. LinkedIn is the place for professionals who want to be recognized and start networking.

Another great tool is InfoUSA, which I use all the time. You can use InfoUSA to target a specific niche. Let's say you want to know where all of the attorneys are in Washington state or a specific city (such as Seattle). You want to know where all the attorneys are who make $500,000 annually, have over five employees, and spend over $200,000 in advertising per year. You can even narrow it down by the zip code and postal walks.

InfoUSA has awesome targeting capabilities, and you can do all of this preparatory research for free. The site will tell you the number of results in a particular market niche, so if you want to purchase those leads, you can get that list. Then you can use that contact information to start to promote your product or services to them. It's a great tool for research; even if you're not going to purchase leads, you will get an idea of how many people are in your niche in a specific city.

Action #42: Use B2C Resources

B2C is business-to-consumer marketing. If you're selling a product or service to consumers rather than businesses, chances are you can find people on Facebook who will be interested. With over 1.49 billion active users as of the year 2015, the targeting capabilities on Facebook are enormous. There is massive opportunity for B2C marketing because Facebook is still such a new platform that can be used for connecting with consumers. If you have the time to keep up with the changes, test and track your efforts, and be creative, then this is hands down the best source around. If you don't have a company profile on Facebook yet, now is a great time to get started.

Action #43: Add to Your Online Methods of Finding People

Facebook, Google AdWords, LinkedIn, and YouTube are all great ways of connecting with your ideal customers. Set up your Facebook page, promote your business to a specific target market on Facebook, and start running Google AdWords campaigns to promote specific services.

Although Facebook is better for B2C than B2B marketing, it sometimes isn't the best approach. One of the companies I consult for is a large tree removal business that does tree chipping, stump removals, etc. We tried getting them on Facebook, but even though it's a B2C site, it didn't work for that company. Most people who need a service (such as tree removal) will leave Facebook and search Google for a specific provider who will help them. We've gotten better results using Google AdWords than on Facebook, even though it is a business-to-consumer company. You just have to test it and see what works for you.

The next thing to consider after discovering where you should market your services is how you should run your advertising campaign. When trying to find their target market and get the best possible response, people often run a bunch of ads online and then say, "It doesn't work," and give up on that online approach.

The truth is, though, that it does work; you just didn't do it right. Figure out what the right market is and where those people are before getting your ads in front of them. Create the right message that will allow them to relate to what you're offering.

The same thing goes for LinkedIn and YouTube: you can run B2B ads on LinkedIn and run newsfeed ads there to promote your services. If you wanted to go after all of those C.E.O.s or attorneys that we talked about in Seattle, you can do the exact same thing on LinkedIn: put an ad right in front of them and target that specific market in that specific area.

The idea here is to prevent wasting hundreds or thousands of dollars on advertising that doesn't communicate your message to the right audience or that is otherwise ineffective. Here's a typical scenario. Most people think of doing newspaper advertising first, and the newspaper ad reps will tell you, "We have a distribution of 240,000." The business owner will get excited and say, "Well, that's great! Two hundred and forty thousand people are going to see my message. My ad cost is going to be $1,000; that's a steal of a deal!"

But you need to think about how many of those people are actually looking for your service. How many of those people are actually going to pick up that newspaper and read that section? I would say 10 percent, nowadays, if not less. But it also depends on your particular area. You have to try different methods and continue testing and tracking your results to see what works. Marketing is not a "set it and forget it" type of activity. You need to be active consistently to get the best results.

It's not just about the number of people who you try to reach. What's more important is contacting people who are going to be interested in your product or service. For example, if you're a weight-loss clinic owner who is focused on getting more weight-loss patients, then ask the advertising rep, "Can you tell me how many people that actually read this paper are overweight? Because that's all I care about: how many people I can reach that are actually looking for what I have to offer them." The more specific you are and the better the questions you ask your advertising reps or marketing people, the better the results you'll have.

Action #44: Determine Where Your Customers Are Offline

If you're thinking of sending direct mail, most people go to their postal service and say, "I want to send my postcard to these 5,000 homes or businesses." A month later, they're wondering why that campaign bombed. The reason why people get poor results from direct mail (a response of less than 0.5 percent, these days) is they're not targeting the right group or sending the right message to the right people.

Prior to creating a campaign, do your research. Find out how many people in your specific area want to do business with you or purchase your product or service. You can narrow it down by targeting a specific area; locate exactly where your ideal customers are instead of just guessing.

Most business owners send a message to all 10,000 people in their area, which is a waste of resources—most of those people won't be interested in your product or service. They just don't need or want it, or even may not be able to afford it. Send your message specifically to those who you know have some level of interest. If you send the right marketing piece to the right people, which will be a smaller number of people, you'll get a better response rate. Your messaging will be specific, clear, and applicable to that target group.

Doing research before you get started helps you to connect with your target market. For example, we did a campaign directed at attorneys. I started looking for attorneys in the western United States and Western Canada who make over $750,000, have over two employees, and spend over $100,000 in advertising. Initially, my list included 3,500 to 4,000 attorneys. But once I started to be more specific and plug in additional traits of my ideal customer, I reduced the list to 97 attorneys. Those 97 attorneys are the people who I wanted to deal with, because I knew that they could afford my services and were looking for a solution to their needs.

When you deal with a specific segment of the market, you quickly realize that most of these prospects will have the same issues. I crafted my packages and promotions with that group of 97 attorneys in mind. It took less effort than targeting a random segment of the population and the reward was much greater.

I researched everything about that group of attorneys. After researching their problems and issues, I zeroed in on the pain points and then crafted my message. I created a strikingly impressive package designed only for this group.

While my competition would blast messages blindfolded, trying to be everything to everyone, I took a different approach. I outdid my competition and I got rewarded handsomely for it. We had an unheard of response rate that exceeded 18 percent.

Likewise, you can find greater success by reducing the number of people that you are contacting. Focus on a smaller group and not only will it take less effort to get the word out, but you will also have a greater percentage of callbacks.

Question #12: How Will You Get Your Prospects' Attention?

This section of element three is where we will be using much of what we discussed in the previous element.

Action #45: Create Your Offer

Create an offer that gets people to raise their hand and say, "Yeah, I'd be interested in that." Businesses usually try to sell prospects on the first go, which is why their marketing has very limited success. Imagine getting thirty or forty different post-cards, direct mail pieces, or advertisements a day, all with people selling you stuff. You're not going to read any of them and decide, "Yes, that's *exactly* what I need!" if it's the first time you've heard of them or the first time you've considered that type of product or service.

People don't want to be sold to. The purpose of direct marketing should be to educate and train your target market on what's happening in their industry, not go for the hard sell. You want prospects to basically agree that, "Yes, this is a big issue in our industry, and I'd love to learn more about it."

Aim to generate interest, not an instant sale. If you reach prospects who become intrigued by your offering, they can contact you to get more information, and you can take the sale from there. But if you try to sell to them right away, you're trying to do something too quickly.

It takes time for people to decide that there is a problem, that they want a solution, and, finally, that they will be seeking that solution from you. Let them come to you, rather than being the pushy salesman who ignores the signs that they aren't ready to sign up for your product or service. Educate them, give them what they're looking for, and you'll be rewarded for it.

Action #46: Create Your Educational Materials

Create educational materials, which may include free training programs, podcasts, free reports, webinars, etc. Get as many things out there that educate your target prospects as you can. Craft specific materials that support your message when you're addressing the problems that your ideal clients have. That gives them an opportunity to learn more from you, which helps to position you as an expert (as opposed to a salesperson).

Creating your educational materials could also involve making a quick-start guide, training video, or even a series of training videos. You don't need to have a huge production team to do that. You can have someone hold your iPhone while you stand in front of a whiteboard and train people on specific topics.

When you create these assets, remember that the purpose of distributing these is to build your status as an industry expert in the eyes of your ideal customers. Your prospects and customers are going to come back and look to you for advice. Maybe they won't buy your services right away, but eventually, if you do a good job of continuously providing value, they will ask you for something or get a free consultation, which will lead them to purchase what you're offering. Essentially, you can presell your prospects and train them on how you do business by educating them. This is something the competition does **not** do.

Action #47: Create Your Marketing Wheel & Circulate Your Educational Materials

Distribute your free educational materials in places where your ideal client hangs out. Advertise in the right areas or through the right outlets, and you will greatly expand your reach. Consider using LinkedIn, attending chamber of commerce meetings or trade shows, and doing a direct mail campaign. If you don't do any of that right now, even trying one of those things can have a positive effect on your business.

After you've created your plan for getting the word out, create a marketing wheel. A marketing wheel is basically a chart that lists options for marketing your product or service (see above image). Start to distribute your free educational materials where people will find them. Post your materials on Facebook, YouTube, LinkedIn, and you will start to become known as the industry expert who everybody goes to.

Action #48: Use Your Assets to Build Trust & Position Yourself as the Authority

Remember, you're not trying to make a sale immediately. At this stage, you're using educational-based marketing, which means you're letting your customers approach you once they're ready. You can stand out from the competition by being the one who provides prospects and customers with greater value through offering these educational materials for free. Distributing those materials will encourage people to choose you.

This is particularly important if you're offering a high-end product or service; people will learn to trust you based on the knowledge that you are freely sharing, and they will be more likely to choose you over the competition. Offering these free educational materials is the most important action in terms of creating and positioning yourself as an expert in your niche. Prospects will look at what you're offering and say, "Man, this guy is giving me all of this valuable information for free. I can't wait to see what he's going to do when I hire him."

Question #13: How Do You Follow Up with Prospects?

Action #49: Position an Appropriate Call-to-Action

You have to do more than just create free educational materials. Eventually, you must have an offer that your prospects can consider accepting. Remember, the end goal is to get clients to come in and do business with you. To do this, you need an appropriate call-to-action that will appeal to your target audience.

For example, you can offer a free 15-minute consultation. Detail exactly what you will be offering in that free consultation, and then assign a value to it. If you do a good job in your educational materials, prospects will know that 15 minutes of your time is an immense value to them.

The formula for your free materials should be as follows:
- Eighty percent educational content

- Ten percent your sales message and call-to-action

- Ten percent cross-marketing promotion (other people's products or services)

If a consultation doesn't fit what you are ultimately offering, then you can offer to give away free samples of your product. Invite your prospects to visit the office for a free training session, try a new piece of equipment for free, etc.

For example, if you are a graphic designer, you can offer free business cards with an original logo design. If you are the owner of a day spa, you can offer a free 25-minute massage (which will get your prospects to purchase a package of 60- or 90-minute massages). If you are an interior decorator, you can offer a free design for one room (which leads prospects to ask you to use that design and do other rooms in their house).

You need to research and figure out what works best for your audience. I've tried hundreds of different offers, and some work great while others don't. If you're not getting any bites from your offer, adjust what you're offering or the way that you're offering it.

Action #50: Follow Up on Your Call-to-Action

Many people have a website where they'll have five or ten different offer types, but that doesn't work; it just confuses the consumer and overwhelms them with too many choices. That's why, in the end, they will often leave the website rather than deciding on an offer. Your call-to-action should be a single, specific offer.

A landing page is a great way to guide people from the educational materials that you've created—your free business videos or quick-start guides—and bring them an offer without confusing them. Get that specific call-to-action out there and don't confuse your prospects with any other calls-to-action. If you're on a budget, Google "free landing page creator"—if you have some money, consider hiring a developer to create this landing page for you. I use a service called LeadPages, and it works great for me.

Do the same thing with your website and social media pages. Clearly define on your website what you want the user to do. Don't just throw a whole bunch of information out there. Design the site to encourage users to follow a specific set of steps.

For example, you might create a clear set of steps that will lead them to download your free training guide, "The Seven Mistakes That Most People Make When Doing X, Y, and Z," or three series of training videos. From there, they will go back to your site a second time and look for the next step, which could be finding further resources or actually purchasing your offering.

Include clearly visible phone numbers if you're in a service business and you want people to call, especially if it's an emergency service business. I can't believe how many times I've seen websites that don't even have a phone number located on the homepage; you've got to search through five different pages just to find their phone number.

Be very direct and specific, and keep in mind that the end goal of creating all these things is to get a customer. Make it incredibly easy for prospects to contact you and get what they need. Your homepage should include your business phone number in large font, and if you provide service for people at your location, then add your address there as well (also in large font).

Action #51: Respond to Online or Offline Leads

A study done at M.I.T. showed that a lead that was responded to within five minutes has a 22 times greater chance of being converted into a paying customer. Did you read that? **Twenty-two times!** Nobody wants to wait to talk to someone from a business; they want to get in touch with someone right away to get their problem solved.

I can't tell you how many times I've seen people have all the right elements, but when somebody picks up the phone, the prospect is sent to voicemail and gets no response for 24 or 48 hours. Even worse, sometimes you go to their website and complete their form, but they never get back to you. I always ask my clients, "How fast do you follow up?" They say, "Oh, usually within 24 hours." I tell them that is not good enough. If you want to double or even triple your business, then call your prospects back within five minutes.

You can't have that delay online. Think about this for a second. When you are searching for something online and you go to someone's website and complete a form asking for more information, what would you normally do next? You will click on the "back" button or go back to Google.com and search for that same type of service. You are in the mindset of finding that service provider immediately.

From your perspective as a business owner rather than a consumer, you know that you need to prevent prospects from seeking your service type elsewhere. Prospects are not going to wait 24 hours for you to get back to them. This is a big problem with most businesses, and most consumers know they can't trust businesses to call them back when they complete a form. All the time, their requests for more information are ignored.

Now, imagine if you call the person within five minutes: you will have taken them away from their search online, started a conversation, and possibly secured an appointment or estimate. Try this in your own business. Nine times out of ten, you'll get that appointment.

When somebody Googles a tree removal business because a tree has fallen on their garage and they need somebody right away, they're going to need someone right away, not 24 hours later. You've paid for advertisements, you've positioned yourself correctly, but this system doesn't work if there's nobody on the other end answering the phones or replying to emails. This is why most businesses fail online. It's not because online marketing doesn't work, it's because their systems on the back end are faulty.

If this side of the business is not working well, stop wasting money on ads. Instead, train your staff to answer the phones, respond to online requests immediately, and use scripts. Train your staff regularly and make sure there's always somebody who will answer the call or respond to instant messaging live. That will increase your revenue—guaranteed.

Action #52: Get a Commitment & Establish an Offline Buying Position

Getting a commitment could require scheduling a time for an assessment or a quote. You're sending out your service provider or getting someone to commit to scheduling an appointment.

When you're trying to get people to commit, make sure that there's a sense of scarcity and urgency there. Get people booked in immediately and let them know that it's important to keep their appointment because other people are also waiting for an appointment.

After someone picks up the phone and calls you, or chats with a representative online and schedules an appointment, they will end the phone call or turn off their computer and say, "Well, I've got my appointment; I have other things to do now." They have chosen to do business with you, so most prospects will not keep shopping around; they're busy and they're going to then go about their day.

But until that person has booked an appointment, they're going to go from business to business, searching for an answer to their problem. If it's an emergency, whoever answers the phone or immediately replies to their email inquiries gets their business (unless you offend the prospect or do something else to turn them away).

You need to schedule their appointment and make sure that they know the time frame and the value of what you're going to provide. Stress the importance of keeping their appointment; tell them that if they cancel, you don't know when you can reschedule. That promotes a feeling of scarcity, which can push them towards making the decision to choose you rather than backing out. Getting your customers to make a commitment is crucial.

Question #14: How Do You Get Your Clients in the Door?

Action #53: Build the Value & Need in Your Service or Product

Stress the value of the service they are about to receive, even if it's free. Emphasize the importance of the service or product that they've committed to, and ensure that your clients keep their appointment. You don't necessarily have to do anything different to increase the value of your offering; sometimes, it's a matter of presenting your offer in a way that speaks to your clients.

It can be as simple as using the right key words to spark their interest. Use words in your ad copy that resonate with your clients; something as simple as changing "class" to "workshop" can have a positive result. That's because while "class" implies that participants will mostly be listening to a lecture and taking notes, "workshop" implies that there will be more interaction from participants (which makes learning easier and more interesting), it will be an event in which their concerns are addressed, and they will potentially have a chance to network with others afterwards.

Action #54: Increase the Likelihood of Your Clients Actually Coming In

Just because they said "Yes" doesn't mean that you have them. They are less likely to back out, but you should still use reminders, phone calls, or emails to keep them engaged. Maybe they don't know what to expect at the appointment or assessment, so ensure that they're consistently engaged with your business until that time. Let them know what they can expect from the appointment or assessment. Consistent follow up is key to reducing no-shows.

Action #55: Automate the Follow-Up Sequence

Following up with your prospects after they schedule an appointment can be easily automated. Create a simple system that your staff can use to send those reminders or further educate the prospect about what they will be getting from that appointment.

Remember, just because they said, "Yeah, I'll come in," that doesn't necessarily mean they're going to actually do so. Some people will talk to their friends or family, who might direct them to a cheaper company or one that they go to. Then you'll get the call where they will say, "Sorry, but I found another person."

To avoid that, you must reaffirm that they're making a good choice and that this is the definite next step for them to take. Remember, there's no business being done until they're in your office. Your main focus should be using systems to ensure they actually show.

Action #56: Leave Nothing to Chance

Build the hype prior to your prospect arriving at your office. Send them portfolios, a link to your business reviews, and/or a short training video on what to expect. You can send information that will help them to get the best experience—perhaps a free gift shipped to their door—which solidifies your position as an industry expert who cares about their business.

Question #15: How Do You Convert Prospects into Clients?

Action #57: Establish Your Prospects' Need for Your Products or Services via a Presentation

If you did a good job in the previous chapter at figuring out what your ideal clients need solutions to, and you've created your free educational materials, the next step is to make a top-notch presentation. It's like a show, and you've got to be on top of your game. Don't just go in there and wing it; craft a plan for this specific presentation.

Action #58: Create Appealing Packaging & Pricing Options

Packaging and pricing options can be the difference between getting a client and almost getting a client. If you've done a good job, your clients will feel as though they can't afford not to purchase your products or services. Make sure that your packaging is solid and that you're presenting your pricing options in an appealing way. Create a three-tier type of package to give your prospects options.

The best example I can give is the time-share industry. If you want to learn how to sell, then go to a time-share presentation. Those guys are rock stars. Back in my real estate days, my training for new salespeople included sending them to a time-share presentation. At a time-share presentation, they'll give you awesome pricing options and they'll justify everything that they do. If you say no on the first pricing option, they'll give you a second pricing option. If you say no to that one, they'll give you a third. They'll keep you there until you say yes.

Offer different pricing options for different people. Likewise, you want to create those different pricing and packaging options. If you have three tiers of pricing options, that's a great start. Try offering a gold, platinum, and titanium option; or an M.V.P., M.V.P. Gold, and M.V.P. Platinum. Usually, if you have those three options, nobody wants to take the cheapest option. Probably 99 percent of the people who you put those pricing options in front of won't take that first least expensive option. They'll either take the middle one or the most expensive one. Nobody wants to be at the bottom of the barrel.

You'll come across people who will always want the best, and you'll come across people who are fine with a mediocre solution. So you want to make sure that the packaging, pricing options, and the affordability are staged and presented well. Increase the revenue in your business by creating three different options. If you only have one option right now, split it into three options. Make the first option not-so-good, make the second option so-so good, and make the third option the best.

I tell clients, "This first option, you're not going to get much out of, to be honest." So I just scratch out that option in front of them and say, "Based on what we talked about and what your experiences are, this option is not good for you. Let's see what these better options can do for you." Lead that conversation into what you feel is best for your client. Remember, they're coming to you for advice. They've seen all of your educational materials, and now they're ready for more and are eager for you to continue to guide them.

Action #59: Offer Financing Options for Affordability

Provide more affordable options, such as a payment plan or a discount. If you have relationships with banks and you sell high-end items, you can offer financing through the bank, too, or do your own in-house financing, offering two-pay or three-pay solutions. Have several different options; you don't want price preventing people from taking advantage of your products or services. When pricing your products, you should not label it as a price, cost, or fee. It should always be presented as an investment. The word "investment" indicates an anticipated return, while the words "cost," "price," and "fee" are seen as money they will not get back.

Action #60: Ask for the Sale & Handle Any Objections

Often, if you go into a business, they'll just hand out information, say, "Okay, well let us know if you want to do business with us," and then let you leave their office. What they should be doing is asking you outright whether you're interested. Don't be like those businesses; tell your prospects, "So, can we do business today? Do you want to put that on Visa or MasterCard? For some of you, this may be hard to do. Let's do this."

That's all you have to do: just ask for the sale and get started. You've shown the prospect your information and an example of your products or services; all that's left is to make the sale.

You may encounter objections such as, "I don't know if I can afford it." That's when you can use take-away selling, which is basically removing those options and saying, "The best thing we have to offer maybe isn't for you." Offer a less expensive service that has fewer perks. It's better to offer a downgrade of a service than to shrug your shoulders and lose the prospect.

All the time, people tell me, "Well, I know a guy who can do it for X amount." I tell them, "Well, that's great. In fact, I probably know three other guys who can do it even cheaper than that, but you get what you pay for." That makes people think, "Man, this guy doesn't need my business," or "Great; he's providing me with different options so I can go somewhere else." It makes them start to think about the decision they're about to make. They might choose you in the end once they realize that it's not about price—it's about value, and you provide greater value than your competitors. That's how you win.

Element #3 Conclusion

This third critical element gave you tons of tools and techniques that you can use to connect with your ideal customers and bring in more business. From expanding your reach across a variety of forms of communication (including social media and traditional postcard mailers) to crafting an appealing pricing system that encourages clients to spend more, in this chapter, we explored a number of possibilities for grabbing your customers' attention and closing sales.

Something as simple as using (or honing) a referral program can also help you to build your customer base; we looked at several ideas for that, as well. Following up is often the key to converting a potential client to a paying customer, and in the next chapter, we will learn how to expand that by upselling and cross-selling, which could be the most lucrative marketing strategies that your business uses. Read on to discover, in depth, how valuable each of your clients may be and why realizing that is crucial to your success.

ELEMENT #4:
MAKE MONEY WITH
UPSELLS & CROSS-SELLS

"Always deliver more than expected."
—Larry Page

This fourth chapter will show you how incredibly valuable each of your customers may be, and what lessons you can take from knowing that worth. Learn to speak your customers' language, so to speak, and add to the value of your offering. Find out why forming good business relationships with people in different industries can exponentially boost your business, and how to approach other business owners. Develop your marketing strategy to help you maintain a strong following in social media and other avenues.

Remember, you should also be focusing on adding to the quality and relevance of your products and services as you continue working on your business. This fourth critical element to building a successful business and ideal lifestyle guides you through the following five questions:

- Question #16: How do you respect the lifetime value of a client and ensure that clients measure up?

- Question #17: What other services do your clients need that you can offer?

- Question #18: Do you have a referral program in place, and is it working?

- Question #19: Which joint-venture partners could bring in more money for your business?

- Question #20: How can you engage people in your business via internal marketing?

This is the chapter to pay the most attention to, because you're going to need all of these tools to expand your business and bring in the type of clients that you want to work with the most. Keep reading to discover how to craft an all-encompassing marketing strategy that will bring the results you've always dreamed of.

Question #16: How Do You Respect the Lifetime Value of a Client & Ensure That Clients Measure Up?

Action #61: Calculate the Lifetime Value of a Customer (It's Not What You Think)

When calculating the value of a customer, let's first consider the customer lifetime value. Predict how much that customer is going to be worth to you in the future if they stick around for X amount of time.

There are many different variables that come into play when calculating a customer lifetime value. Most business owners don't understand this at all. If I ask them, "How much are your customers worth to you?" they look at it from a single transactional point—meaning that if someone comes in and buys a widget from them, they'll tell me that their customer is worth that widget that one time. That small-minded kind of thinking prevents you from accurately assessing the worth of a customer. Instead of looking at a single transaction, you should be monitoring how much that person is bringing in to your business over their lifetime to calculate the potential for that customer.

Once you understand how much profit you will realize from each of your customers, you can absolutely revolutionize the way that you do business. Your customers are probably worth more than you think. For example, if your average sale is $50 and your average customer buys from you four times per year, that's $200 per year per customer. Now, if this customer does business with you, on average, for ten years, then the lifetime customer value becomes $2,000.

But that's not actually the true lifetime customer value. You also have to calculate how much business they are bringing to you; customers who are going to you who, otherwise, would have gone to a competitor or never solved their problem.

Here's an example of how referrals and word-of-mouth can boost your earnings. My wife and I go to the same restaurant about twice a month. Our typical meals come to 30 or 40 bucks per plate. If you calculate that (two visits over the course of 12 months), that's 24 meals that we're going to eat; based on $30 per plate, that's $720 per year each—$1,440 that we spend as a couple. If we go for the next ten years, our buying lifetime is $14,400 in sales.

In the beginning of that ten-year period, let's say we refer ten people to the restaurant because we love it so much. Half of them also love the restaurant, and they have the same or similar spending patterns as we do.

Maybe those five people join us for dinner, go by themselves, or even bring their wives to hang out there twice a month for the next ten years. At one plate per referral, that's an additional $3,600 per year (of course, if they always bring their wife, that doubles it to $7,200 per year). In ten years, that's $36,000—or $72,000 if they always bring someone else with them.

If you add the $14,400 that we will spend in ten years to the $36,000 that we generated through recommending our friends to the restaurant, that boosts our customer value from a $30 plate to the real value of more than $50,000. If our friends routinely bring someone else to dine with them, that's more than $85,000 that we're bringing in over ten years!

That's a huge increase. It's important for us to know what the value is of each customer, because it's not just about that one meal or even that second meal for their dinner date; it's about the course of their lifetime and how many people they're going to refer.

Take a moment now to calculate your lifetime customer value using my downloadable worksheet. Download your Lifetime Customer Value spreadsheet calculator and other money-making resources at www.BobMangat.com/Book-Offer.

Action #62: Love Your Customers More

Knowing the numbers, you know your customer is not worth 30 bucks; they can be worth over $85,000. How good are you going to treat them, just by knowing their real customer lifetime worth? It's a completely different ballgame once you've done this exercise in the previous action. You start taking care of them more, maybe offering them free meals, and maybe giving them free dessert to build customer loyalty (or the equivalent in your industry).

Depending on your industry, you can usually start to create a VIP status to reward your loyal customers. Airlines are a great example of this: the more you fly, the more rewards you earn, because they understand that the longer you stick around, the more you will spend and the more you will refer others to them. This past year, I've flown maybe 100,000 or 120,000 miles. I fly mostly with Alaska Airlines because it's close to me and it hits up all 50 states or wherever else I want to go. I reached a different tier in their rewards system. Now, they have given me a specific VIP concierge phone number to call; I don't have to wait in line. I can go and use their boardroom and hang out in their lounges.

I get upgraded all the time to first class, and I get preferred rates when I fly Alaska. Now, do you think I'm going to go and book a flight anywhere else? Even if I get charged $100 less through different last-minute sites, I still see the value in what Alaska is going to give me, so I'm still going to fly with them. They treat me like royalty, and rightfully so: I spend a lot of money with them. They understand this concept and reward frequent fliers with these perks, knowing what the value is to them.

Once you know your customer's lifetime worth to your business, start creating a program to reward your customers to get them to bring more customers in. Then, make sure that you take care of your customers so they will remain loyal to your business.

Action #63: Budget for Customer Acquisition

If you know now that I'm worth over $50,000 to $85,000 to your business over the course of ten years, what will you pay to acquire me? What will you pay to get me to come to your restaurant? Is it $100? $200? $1,000? $2,000? What can you afford to pay?

I've been in the real estate business for a long time. I'm not in real estate anymore, but I remember when people would spend 50 percent of their commission on referral agreements to acquire more clients.

For example, if I referred somebody out to somewhere else on the other side of the country, we would get a check back for 50 percent of the commission. Sometimes it would be 25 percent; sometimes it would be 50 percent. You ask them, "Hey, why don't you run some ads or do some marketing? Rather than paying 50 percent or $5,000 or $6,000, you can probably acquire a customer for $1,000."

But they won't spend that much right at the beginning; they're relying on referrals to build their business. Not only that, they're spending more money to get those people than if they understood these concepts in this book and created strategic marketing campaigns.

Referrals are fine, and you need to get referrals when you can, but that is a very slow-growth model. If you budget your money to be able to afford a marketing campaign, you will usually see much faster results. Remember, add multiple pillars to your business to create exponential growth.

Action #64: Act & Think Like the Big Boys

Look at how much money you can afford to spend on customer acquisition. This is where the big boys know precisely what they're doing. Back in the day, I did affiliate marketing; some companies would pay me anywhere from $150 to $500 per qualified lead. They didn't have to do business with the company for me to get paid; they just needed to apply for an insurance quote, or something like that.

They were willing to spend that much per lead because they knew their conversion rates and the lifetime value of their customers. They figured, "If we can spend $1,500 to get five applications, one of those leads will become a client, and we will make X amount from that person."

It just made sense for them to invest that much per lead because of the huge payoff, especially for a company that's in the insurance industry. Chances are if they insure your car, they'll get your home, critical illness, life, education savings plans, and more. They know their numbers, and so should you.

Business owners need to be looking at investing in acquiring customers. That's what the big boys do: they buy customers. If they were to just focus on referrals, they would never be at the level that they're at. Their main thing is, "How many people can we buy?"

The ratio of the customer's lifetime value to the cost of acquiring that customer depends on the business. If you're a smaller business—such as if you run a restaurant that only makes an average of $20 per plate—you're not going to invest $500 or $1,000 in a customer, since you won't see a return until the third, fourth, or fifth year.

Don't spend all of your money on customer acquisition costs, especially if the return is too far in the future and/or is shaky (you don't know that that customer will love your restaurant enough to return every month or refer friends). You need to pull in a profit, and that means using your budget for customer acquisition in the most effective ways possible.

If you spend $150 on acquiring a $20 customer right away, then you had better be sure that you know your numbers. If they are only spending $20 with you, then this scenario won't work. If you're not doing a good job on the back end on selling them other products or services, then this will be a problem for you.

Start keeping track of what your customers spend with you over the next couple of months to figure what you can afford to spend on customer acquisition. (We'll get more into upselling in the next action.) Another possibility is beginning the referral process sooner so you can start to get more people in and recover your customer acquisition costs quicker.

Question #17: What Other Services Do Your Clients Need That You Can Offer?

Action #65: Upsell

An upsell is just that: something that you sell to customers that is more expensive than what they were initially going to buy. It can be an upgrade or other add-on items that increase the value of the original product or service they wanted.

If you buy a book on Amazon—let's say you want to buy <u>Rich Dad, Poor Dad</u>—once you add that to your cart, Amazon will say, "Bob, get $80 off instantly upon approval for the Amazon.com Rewards Visa Card." Right away, they're asking you to sign up for their store card.

Then, as you scroll down the page, Amazon shows you products in these categories: "Items from Your List" (your wish list), "Buy It Again" (recently purchased items), "Recommendations for Items from Across Our Store" (recommendations based on purchase history), and "Frequently Bought with <u>Rich Dad, Poor Dad</u>" (similar products). They'll try to upsell you on a little bit more to increase your value as their customer.

That's a case of recommending add-ons; an upgrade example of upselling is buying fries and then being asked, "Do you want to super-size those fries?" Another example is buying ten sessions with a personal trainer in a package deal instead of buying only a single session.

Action #66: Cross-Sell

An example of a cross-sell is buying a Big Mac combo at McDonald's and then being asked, "Do you want an apple pie with that?" A cross-sell is selling to an existing customer, whether that's a different product or a different service.

A cross-sell is something that can either increase your profits by providing other solutions or products that can help the customer. Apple is a cross-selling genius; they will sell you an Apple care protection plan with your new laptop.

Another example of cross-selling is a chiropractor offering supplements, orthotics, and/or massage therapy in addition to their chiropractic services. I just got off the phone with a guy that sells mattresses in his chiropractic office; that's a premium upsell product.

Action #67: Add Upsells & Cross-Sells

McDonald's doesn't make any money on the hamburgers that they sell you for $1.99 or so. They're making their money on the drinks that you upsize, which are very cheap for them because it's just sugar and water. They try to upsell your fries, too. Their initial offerings don't generate much profit alone, so upselling and cross-selling is where they make the bulk of their profits.

For your business, that's likely where your profits are as well: once you start to add upsells and cross-sells, you can start to see an impressive difference in the money you're generating. For example, if you're a personal trainer, then offering a ten-pack of training sessions at a discount might be an option. Not only will your client save money, but it also gives you more income to put back into your business right away since they're buying in bulk in one payment.

Action #68: Sell Other People's Products (Cross-Marketing)

Another form of cross-marketing is selling other people's products. An example of this is a chiropractor selling mattresses. If you aren't upselling or cross-selling your own products or services, selling other people's products can be a great way to complement what you're offering. Check out other industries and see whether anyone has products that you can sell alongside your own products. It can work in your favor in a number of ways; a client might actually be interested in other people's products that you're selling, and once they purchase that, you can then talk to them about your own products.

Question #18: Do You Have a Referral Program in Place, & Is It Working?

Action #69: Harness the Power of Referrals

When you get a referral, you're likely to do business with that person, which is why referrals are powerful. Referrals come from a recommendation by a trusted source. That means you don't have to sell them on your products or services as much.

For example, if a family member referred me to a doctor, I probably wouldn't research other doctors or look elsewhere. I'd schedule an appointment, trusting in the good experience that my family member had with that doctor.

Getting referrals means you don't have to convince those clients of what you're offering. Read the next action step to learn how to get more referrals.

Action #70: Learn to Increase Referrals

I always get asked, "How can I get more referrals?" Most of the time, people are reactive, meaning they'll ask the client, "Do you know of anybody who might be able to use our services?" And they'll say, "Yeah." Then the business owner will say, "Okay, great; we'd appreciate it if you'd send them our way."

Nine times out of ten, though, that person won't give you those promised referrals. You have to actively promote them instead of waiting for someone else in your network to make that connection.

My chiropractor asked me, "Hey, when are you going to bring your family members in?" I said, "Whenever you ask me to." He said, "Okay, well, here are the forms; have your wife fill these out, and bring her in." I'm a busy guy, and I didn't do it. I forgot. He should have taken the phone number and called my wife or my family members to ask them to come in.

I told my chiropractor that—I said, "Well, why didn't you just take the phone number and call them?" On the same day that he called, he scheduled an appointment with my wife, who is now a regular at that chiropractic clinic with a first-year value of $2,500. All that with one phone call. But it took almost three months for that to happen, because he had spent all that time waiting for me to promote his services.

Ask for the referral and then have a member of your staff follow up with a phone call. Have your secretary say, "So-and-so told us to give you a call, and we just wanted to see if you could come in for a consultation." Calling those referrals immediately will amplify the number of referrals doing business with you sooner.

Action #71:
Create a Reason for Clients to Refer You

Word of mouth is not enough to generate referrals. Find a reason why people should refer you. Incentivize people to bring referrals in; maybe they'll get a free T-shirt, a free consultation, or a free upgrade to the next service package for a month. Create a referral program: if you refer X number of people, you get this.

In our business, we have different tiers within our referral program. At three referrals, at seven, at ten, and at fifteen referrals, we have different rewards.

At three referrals, we might give our clients a $250 Visa gift card. At five referrals, we might give them certain services plus that gift card, or some gift baskets from Omaha Steaks. At ten referrals, we might give them a certain number of services, a gift card, and maybe a nice mini-vacation on us (depending on the client).

You can offer those different tiers within your referral program to get your clients started or to provide them with incentives. If you don't know what to offer, simply ask them what they would like for referring someone to your business.

Action #72: Don't Wait to Ask for Referrals: Ask When a Client Signs Up

Ask your clients for referrals right away when they sign up and become a client or patient. Usually, business owners will wait until their new client has had some success with their services or until they have seen their client for three or four months (or however long it takes to start seeing some changes). Don't wait for a success story. On the first day when your client is signing up, they're excited and they're ready to go. That's the ideal time to ask them, "Do you know anybody else who might be interested in a free consultation?"

When I went to the time-share presentation and bought that time-share. I hadn't even taken one vacation yet before they put a form in front of me and said, "Open up your phone and tell me who you think might be interested in getting a free vacation." I said, "Well, a free vacation? I know a lot of guys that would do that."

So they got me to open up my phone and write down ten names and numbers of people, my family and friends—remember, I hadn't had any experience with any of their properties yet. That was almost seven years ago. To this day, they're still calling those same people that haven't come in for their free vacation.

This is how relentless you need to be in your referral process. Asking for referrals right away is a very proactive move; you know that if you can get more clients to come in, you can take it from there and sell them on your products and services.

Question #19: Which Joint-Venture Partners Could Bring in More Money for Your Business?

Action #73: Collaborate with Businesses That Complement Yours

Create relationships with other businesses that offer services or products that your clients may need. For example, if you are a chiropractor and you don't have a massage therapist in your office, consider making a joint-venture partnership with a licensed massage therapist.

It's a very simple concept: "You refer business to me, and I'll refer business to you." If there's a certain product that your customers are consistently asking for, go out there and search for a partner who specializes in that product. Make a deal with them: "I'll send you people, and you can send me people as well." Make that relationship.

Download the complete joint venture blueprint at www. BobMangat.com/Book-Offer.

You can keep those products in-house (within your business). Or, you can refer clients to your joint-venture partners and say, "Hey, I know a guy that would do that; check out his business," and give them some marketing materials for your joint-venture partner's business, along with the contact info.

Action #74: Reach Out to Leaders in Your Industry

If there are specific online (or even offline) people who are going to certain events, such as a trusted authority, industry expert, or leader in a particular field, schedule an appointment to tell them your story. You can do a business lunch where you'll tell them a little about yourself, ask to know more about them and what they do, and see if you have synergy.

Leaders always have a huge following, so those are the people you want to reach out to once you're ready. If you look at their profiles on Facebook, LinkedIn, or Instagram, and see how active they are, then you can get your information on their radar and make that connection.

If you can get in with the right industry expert or the right leader, they may have five or six hundred people that they're consistently communicating with (or even more). That's their circle of influence. By joining them and meeting on a regular basis, providing them with what they need (not what you need), you'll then be able to expand your own circle of influence; get them interested in what you're doing, and they'll broadcast that to their following of hundreds of people.

Even better: if they become one of your joint-venture partners, you can make use of their influence, knowledge, and skills. They will be more likely to want to provide you with business advice and tips every once in a while, because if you succeed, their own success increases as well. One good joint-venture partner can make the difference in your business.

Action #75: Create a Referral Process to Get Customers from Those Businesses

How are you going to get customers into your business? It's great that you've made those joint-venture partnerships, but how are you going to get those people who will come into your business and use your services?

Create a process to get those people into your business. Having a systematic process to get those people into your business is key.

For example, I have a chiropractor who we recently built a referral process for: a client can log on to their website and complete a form that is automatically sent to their office. Then the receptionist will call and say, "We know that you're calling from such-and-such a company, a partner of so-and-so, and we want to get you booked in to see the doctor A.S.A.P." All of the activities of that referral partner are tracked, so you know who's sending what over to you. This is important as you start to build your relationship and focus more of your time on the 20 percent that actually sends you the most referrals.

Action #76: Create a Win-Win Strategy: Come from a Place of Service

I hate it when you go to those networking events and people just sit there and pass you cards and say, "Hey, listen, if you—" They don't know that it isn't all about them.

I never go to networking events, but at the few that I've gone to over the years, people will pass you a card and say, "Hey, if you ever need this, let me know." Yet they've never asked me what I do, how they can help me, or how they may put me in touch with somebody that I may need. Coming from a place of service is a lot better than just saying, "Here: this is what I do. Send people over."

There are going to be benefits to those leaders or joint-venture partners as well when you connect with them. Keep in mind that everybody is thinking, "What's in it for me?" If you're always just in it for your own needs or wants, then the relationship won't work.

If you go to networking events, or even if you're contacting someone through a different channel, figure out what they need and focus on that. Find out what their business needs are. Maybe they're struggling with something that you're a pro at, and you can offer to give them some pointers over coffee or lunch. You don't even necessarily want to make any of your own requests when you meet; if you save that for later, they'll be apt to like and trust you, and they won't mind helping you. Make it all about them, not you, especially in the early stages.

Question #20: How Can You Engage People in Your Business via Internal Marketing?

Action #77: Keep Top-of-Mind Awareness (T.O.M.A.)

What are you doing on a regular basis to keep yourself at the top of your customer's mind? First, you should be regularly updating your social media pages with relevant information and answering people's questions about your business on your social media pages. That's usually the fastest and easiest way to start a conversation with your customers online (other than an online chat client, but they would have to visit your website to do that).

If you don't already do one, create an e-newsletter that clients or prospects can subscribe to; send it every two to four weeks. Create value in your newsletters and don't try to sell people on stuff all the time, or they'll unsubscribe.

Another way to remind clients of your services and products is to send the occasional piece of direct mail to them, possibly along with a referral card. Again, just like the e-newsletters, make sure you don't overwhelm your prospects or clients; limit yourself to sending direct mail every three to four weeks or so.

Action #78: Offline Strategies

My dentist sends me a postcard in the mail every six months to remind me about my checkup. It'd probably be better if he didn't send it only every six months when he wanted me to go into his office. If he could send it to me every month about something different each time, that would be more effective.

He knows that I've got two kids; he could send me some stuff on what I need to do in terms of managing my children's health. They have so many other services that they can market: braces, crowns, whitening services; you name it. My dental clinic has different services, but they've never, ever pitched any of them to me other than reminding me of a regular checkup.

What does it cost to send a postcard to one person? Probably 30 or 40 cents. Sending a postcard every six or eight months is just not enough. You need to be able to send it to them on a regular basis. Being there consistently keeps you at the top of your client's mind.

Once a month is a good strategy, whether it's an offer or a reminder. You can send them a postcard letting them know about your new educational video, podcast, etc. The monthly messages can get clients excited and coming back in to spend more with you, and to possibly upsell them to different services.

You can host events with your joint-venture partners to get your customers in on a regular basis. It doesn't have to be something huge; it can be something that's in your office that's timely and critical, whatever it may be. That helps you to consistently keep your business on their mind.

Action #79: Use Online Strategies like Facebook, Email Lists, & Monthly Newsletters

This ties in with keeping your business in front of your prospects and clients. People have a natural inclination to wander and look elsewhere if you don't stay in their mind. Doing a good job at providing your products and services is only part of the equation; you also need to be in front of your customers all the time.

Use social media, e-newsletter subscriptions, and more to spread your message, stay in the front of your customers, and encourage referrals. Asking, "Do you know anybody?" may give you a few names, but it's better to get those messages out through your social media channels and e-newsletters.

Going back to the idea of only working on what you're skilled at and leaving the other jobs to employees, you can hire someone specifically to work on your social media campaigns and another person to field questions from customers and prospects through those channels. Regularly monitoring social media channels also alerts you to any P.R. mishaps, which you can address quickly to prevent a snowball effect.

Action #80: Get More Referrals, More Sales, & the Ability to Sell More Stuff More Often

When you've already invested so much into getting a client, you don't want to lose them to someone else's marketing. Keep marketing to your clients, keep providing them valuable resources for free that complement your products and services, and keep doing more to provide higher quality products and services than the competition.

It's just like marriage: you don't stop dating your wife, and likewise, you don't stop marketing to your clients. Act as though you are still in the stages of winning them over, and you will have a better chance of keeping them interested in what your business can offer them. It doesn't take much to do this, and it all can be automated.

The more clients that you get, the more sales you'll have, along with the ability to sell more stuff. Referrals are one avenue of creating those relationships; then you can move on to creating a system for upselling and cross-selling to increase your lifetime customer value. That creates further stability in your business as well as putting more money in your pocket.

Element #4 Conclusion

In this fourth critical element, we discovered the potential worth of a single client and how you can build customer loyalty to create a longer business relationship with your customers. One of the concepts that we focused on was how you can network with others and start using cross-marketing techniques to offer greater value and provide more solutions for your ideal clients.

Grow your business by making a habit of using these tools and strategies, which will exponentially increase your business. It's not enough to draw from these strategies every once in a while; you need to consistently work on building your business. Make it a habit to upsell, cross-sell, and get your people to call clients and prospects. In the next chapter, you will read about how you can build your dream business and enjoy the ideal lifestyle that you have always wished to live.

ELEMENT #5:
BUILD YOUR DREAM
BUSINESS

*"Twenty years from now you will be more disappointed by the
things that you didn't do than by the ones you did do. So throw off
the bowlines. Sail away from the safe harbor.
Catch the trade winds in your sails. Explore. Dream. Discover."*
—H. Jackson Brown Jr.

In this final chapter, we will discover the secret to bringing in
more income, dealing only with your best clients, and having
more time to spend with your family (rather than working).
Find out how you can make a huge difference in your business
and, ultimately, create a path to stress-free freedom.

This final critical element to building a successful business
and ideal lifestyle guides you through the following five questions:

- Question #21: How does focusing on your profit put
  more in your pocket?

- Question #22: Why should you stop working in your
  business?

- Question #23: How do you leverage people?

- Question #24: How do you leverage time and technology?

- Question #25: How do you create stress-free freedom for yourself in your business?

Once you finish this chapter, you'll have all of the resources that you'll need to realize your dreams and dominate your chosen niche—but just in case, there are a few bonus pages afterwards that you can check out, including a resources page.

Read on to discover precisely how to reach your end goal of running a business that you can be proud of while having plenty of time to enjoy with your family.

Question #21: How Does Focusing on Your Profit Put More in Your Pocket?

Action #81:
Charge Your Clients 25 to 30 Percent More

Chances are, you're charging too little for your services. As you go through this process, you need to always be thinking of your ideal client. Usually, your ideal client can afford your services at the price that you would like to charge.

I tell all of my clients, "You should be charging 25 to 30 percent more." They have a hard time grasping this concept, because they think that they're going to outprice the market so that their competitors will get the business instead—but that's not necessarily the case.

If all of these strategies in this book are done right, charging 25 to 30 percent more won't be an issue. I have a lot of competition in my business; in fact, I get maybe half a dozen calls to the office every week asking me what my price is.

I never tell them. I say, "Well, if you're searching for price, then I'm not the guy for you. In fact, I can give you names of people who you can get dirt-cheap service from." The clients who ask about price are the ones that I don't want. I want the clients who understand the value of what I'm offering: not only will they stick around, but they'll also invest the money that I require.

Your ideal client will look at different businesses, and if they're comparing, they may find someone who's competing on price, someone who is competing from a service aspect, and someone who is competing from a service aspect and a higher price. Win them over by providing high-quality products or services.

People don't mind paying more for what you provide. By charging 25 to 30 percent more than the average service provider, you're avoiding the people with whom you don't want to do business. You will be working with people who are going to value what you do, and even though you may deal with fewer clients, you'll be making more money providing the same service.

Action #82: Stop Competing on Price

Your ideal clients aren't searching Groupon for your products or services. We all know what type of clients use Groupon. They're deal-hunters, most are not loyal, and they're not people who are looking for everything else that you offer. They're not going to be comparing anything; they're going to grab a coupon, grab a deal, and then move on.

They may find that same service elsewhere, and they don't care whether they go to your business or somebody else's. They just want the best deal that they can get; they're not comparing services or products. Let other businesses that don't know these concepts in this book go after those people.

Often, when people are not getting a lot of business, they will run a Groupon promotion and then they'll either get hammered with negative reviews because they can't handle the business, or they'll get people coming in for that one service and that's it (not to mention that you're giving away 50 percent of your revenue on the deal to Groupon).

The supposed methodology behind Groupon is to get people in at a lower cost and try to convert them to a higher-priced product, but only 5 percent—if that much—will be interested in your upselling. Your ideal client is not looking on Groupon to buy things. They're doing their research online or checking out some reviews. They're going to your website and seeing what you're all about, why you're different, and how your products or services differ from everybody else's. They're watching your videos, listening to your podcasts, and reading your e-books. Compete based on the quality of what you're offering, not on price.

Action #83: A 10 Percent Price Increase Can Result in 100 Percent More Profit

With any price increase, you've set up your business for a little bit more profit. Whatever your profit margins are, when you add 10, 15, 20 percent to it, that's all added profit. Slight increases in pricing can normally realize double, triple, or more in terms of profit.

For example, if you've got a $100 product that costs $90 to make, distribute, and advertise, then your profit on one sale is $10, or 10 percent of the customer's price. If you were to charge 10 percent more ($110), your profit would increase by 100 percent.

Often, people will tell me they want to double their business. Their automatic assumption is, "I've got to double the number of people that come in." I tell them, "No, you don't. You can extract money from the people who are already in there."

Think about it: if you doubled your business by actually doubling the number of clients who came into your office, how many people would you have to hire to serve them? Doubling your business in terms of the number of people you serve won't double the profit of your business. Increase profits without increasing expenses or workload by simply raising your prices.

Question #22: Why Should You Stop Working in Your Business?

Action #84: Design Your Lifestyle & Fund It through Profits

From an early age, I've always thought about other people's money or other people's products. To design your lifestyle and fund it through your profits, there are a few guidelines you need to follow. First, if you can't afford to buy something, don't buy it. If you want something, then figure out how many people you need to service and how many more new clients you need to bring in to be able to fund that lifestyle choice—or, as we discussed in the previous action, by what percentage you should raise your prices.

For example, if you want a new car, and that new car will cost you $500 per month for the lease, and your average customer nets you $100 on a monthly basis, then you need five new customers—seven, actually, to account for client drop-off—to be able to fund that vehicle choice.

I've used this principle with real estate, vehicles, and my kids' education fund; I've done it with everything. Plan to use other people's money to buy what you need and to fund your lifestyle of choice. You won't want to dip into your savings and pull that money out, which is what most people do; nor should you want to rely on credit. It might take you five or six months, or even a year, to save the money or get the clients you need, but you will have done it without changing your lifestyle.

Action #85: Work on Your Business, Not in It

Most people are ingrained in the day-to-day mechanics of their business: paperwork, servicing clients, and a host of activities that they do on a regular basis. That's not what a business owner should be doing. That is where the burnout happens and why people aren't passionate about working in their business anymore. They're looking to sell their business (which is probably not worth a whole lot) or do something else, because they're working too much in it.

If you're consistently working in your business 24/7, you're not going to be able to take a step back and look at it. I've dealt with so many people who, on a yearly basis, spend more than what they make. I'll ask them how much they make; they'll tell me $150,000. I'll ask how much they spend, and they'll tell me $150,000 or $170,000. And they've been going on like this for years!

Step away from your business and take a good look at what's going on with it. Be honest with yourself about your financial position. Work on your business, not in it. Determine exactly what's going wrong and why, and then get to work fixing it. Where is profit being left on the table? How can you fix that? Use the systems and strategies that will allow you to afford the lifestyle that you desire.

Action #86: Make Your Business Support the Life That You Want

Make sure that your business is supporting that life you want. I started in the real estate business when I was 22. They told me,

"Go send out flyers and go do some door-knocking. Pick up the phone and cold-call all your friends and do all that kind of stuff." If you know me, I'm not that kind of a person. I said, "There's no way I am going to do that." I tried it once, because I thought that was the way we would be successful in business. I did the regular "retail" real estate side of things is what I call it working with regular home sellers and buyers. I did that for six years, working 80 hours a week, making a couple hundred grand a year but spending a couple hundred grand a year and never having any savings.

Once I started to look at things differently, everything changed for me. I decided, "I need to charge more money, get better clients, and work less."

I saw a huge shift when I started to look at what I wanted my lifestyle to be. I started to plan a little bit for the future, my kids, and what I wanted my life to look like in six months, a year, two years. I charged 30 to 40 percent more money than any other broker in my industry, and most would think it was illegal! No; I provided service and immense value. Every strategy that I'm sharing here in this book has helped me to make more money.

The difference was I provided a different service that was worth it. I believe that, and so did everybody else. Supporting my lifestyle was easy when I had the business I needed. The home that I bought was bought through the real estate profit recurring revenue that I built. So were the cars that I bought; I didn't buy them all at once. It took me six years to build it, but it gave me the lifestyle that I wanted.

Action #87: Design Your Lifestyle

If you don't know what you want or where you're going, how will you get there? I think of that every single day: if I don't know where I'm going tomorrow, or if I don't know where I'm going in six months, how will I get there? I have to plan and find out what I actually want.

Designing your lifestyle is simple. If you look at your business or lifestyle, you will see what needs to change and what doesn't. For the financial aspect, list all of your expenses and discover what else you need to create that ideal lifestyle. Are you going to cut back in some categories to shift your money to things that better serve you, or are you going to boost your earning power instead?

However you choose to work towards your ideal lifestyle, you need a plan. It has to be realistic and you should have daily goals to meet along the way. Five-year plans are popular, but I don't use one; I have a daily plan. I know what I want and where I hope to be in the future, but if I don't make an effort on a daily basis, I'm not going to get there.

I had a coffee with a buddy of mine who told me about his very impressive five-year plan. I said, "That's great, but what are you doing today to get to that five-year plan?" He goes out partying most nights and shows up late to work on a regular basis, but he's got a five-year plan, all right.

If you don't put in the work today and tomorrow for your future—if you don't design your lifestyle, work on your business, create your marketing wheel and marketing programs—then you simply won't achieve your five-year plan. Keep your plan realistic and celebrate small wins. Big wins rarely happen, so don't chase those. Keep hitting those small consistent wins on a regular basis, and eventually, in five years, you will have smashed your original big win.

Action #88: Create Your Ideal Lifestyle

List everything you want in your ideal lifestyle: expenses such as savings, salaries, staffing costs, enrolling your kids in private school, buying a car, taking nice vacations, etc. This isn't about your lifestyle today; this is about your ideal lifestyle. How will you set up your business for maximum growth or for maximum profits that will fund that lifestyle?

Look at everything: the cars that you want to drive and the homes that you want to live in. Visualize your ideal lifestyle. You'll get more out of it if you have daily goals to work on; those goals are what get you to achieve your three- or five-year plan.

List everything that you have and that you want. Reverse engineer how you're going to reach your goals. How many clients will you need per week? How much profit should each one bring? How much money do you need to make each month? What are your business expenses?

Track all of those things so you can create your ideal lifestyle.

Don't have it written down? It ain't going to happen. As Eisenhower said, "...I have always found that plans are useless, but planning is indispensable."

Question #23: How Do You Leverage People?

Action #89: Calculate What You're Worth Hourly

If you can consistently provide the top service that makes you the most amount of money in the least amount of time, use that to calculate your hourly rate. For example, if you're a chiropractor who is adjusting four or five people per hour at fifty bucks a pop, that's $250 to $300 per hour. Anything less than that, you should not be doing, because that would minimize your self-worth. Leave the bookkeeping, the appointment setting, and the cleaning to someone who will work for $10/hour. Outsource your menial tasks and focus on high-dollar value activities instead.

Action #90: Recover Your Hours Wasted on $10/Hour Jobs

What are you doing on a regular basis? Where are you wasting your time, and what tasks can you delegate or outsource? You don't have to dump everything all at once, but consider farming out your low-paying work. Hire the right people to let go of the things that prevent you from focusing your valuable time where you excel.

You might have a hard time letting go, which can be a trust or control issue. It could also be an issue of not knowing where to start: how to delegate, who to hire, or where to find freelancers or contracted employees. Fill that knowledge gap by doing your research and talking with or hiring a consultant to get you to your end goal faster.

Only do what makes you that $250 or $300 per hour, if that's what you're worth. The benefit is you'll spend fewer hours working, you'll get better results and more money, and you'll have more time for setting up and working on your business. Set up the systems or create the job profiles that will help you work more on your business. Create marketing wheels and use your talents. Leave driving to the bank and depositing your checks to your assistant.

Action #91: Hire the Smart Way

Today's technology allows you to hire people for less than $10/hour to do data-entry work or anything like that overseas. There are so many people looking for a job, and they may even accept a training gig. I sponsor a soccer team, which costs me $1,000 per year, but I train and mentor students to do work for me. That gives me four or five months each year in which I have three or four students working for me for free.

You can hire interns, college students, or local high school students looking for an after-school job. If you want to do it, you can get it done. Sometimes you hire the wrong person, but that's when you can see it as a learning experience: ask yourself, "Where did I go wrong? How can I prevent these problems from happening again? Who is my ideal freelancer or contracted employee?" Failing doesn't mean you should give up and decide that outsourcing doesn't work; failing gives you the opportunity to improve your approach and get some talented people working for you.

Use the same strategies that you used to narrow down your ideal client. You want to get ideal workers, so write down your budget, their requirements, desired traits (such as adaptability or speedy service), and where you can find them. Browse through job boards or seek referrals from others who have had a great experience.

Action #92: Set Up Systems for Your Staff (Tracking, Accountability, & Process)

Usually, people will just hire someone and say, "Here, answer the phones." That's it. Then that secretary is going to work just for the paycheck and isn't invested in the company's success. You can easily keep your staff included in the whole process and ensure that they are focused on increasing revenue (perhaps providing incentives for them to do so).

Once you have hired people, you need to set up a system to track what they're doing, monitor progress, and consistently train them to improve their work. Hold a weekly training meeting in which you outline your expectations and hold your staff accountable. Ask for input from your staff; sometimes, a lower-level employee will have a great idea that can save the business thousands in revenue. At the least, you will build loyalty and cultivate an inclusive environment.

Using systems such as customer relationship managers (C.R.M.), email/text marketing, and appointment reminders can be as cheap as a $10 monthly subscription. Teach your staff how to use these systems effectively. Have your receptionist use a tracker for phone numbers, logging calls, or even recording calls from the web to be used for training purposes.

Get C.R.M. software before anything else. If you're in sales, there are some lower-priced options. We use Infusionsoft here. There's Base CRM, Sugar CRM, and PipeDrive for sales (pipeline management), to name a few.

You can get started for $20 or $30 a month. Some systems include accounting and bookkeeping, email marketing, and/or automated follow-up systems. Set up automatic emails that go out to your clients and educate them on certain things; set it up once and you can forget it.

Track your web analytics to see the number of visitors, how many times they visited a certain page, the conversion rate, and more. Engage with your customers via a live chat service. To book appointments, try Vcita, TimeTrade, or Demandforce for a more robust solution. Send S.M.S. reminders with Call Loop.

We use a spreadsheet on our Google Drive to get an overview of how our salespeople are doing: the number of connections, client calls, presentations, and what their closing rate is. Then I evaluate those stats and see whether I'm going to hire more people, fire that person, or aid in training them some more if they're worth it.

Question #24: How Do You Leverage Time & Technology?

Action #93: Some Jobs Just Aren't for People Anymore

Every single time I needed a haircut, I had to call my hairstylist's office to ask about his availability and schedule an appointment. He was in a pretty busy salon, and I wondered how much money was wasted compared with using a system where clients could book their appointments online.

Two weeks ago, my stylist left that place and opened his own shop. Now he uses an app where I can log in 24/7 and find out when his times are—I don't have to call or text him, and my appointment is booked instantly. Using that app has increased his service level and customer satisfaction.

That's just one example of a job that you don't need people for anymore. The list of the things that are managed by technology is endless. Those were all $10 or $15/hour jobs five years ago, but today, they're not. If you haven't embraced these possibilities of expanding your service and reducing administrative costs, give it a test run now.

Action #94: Automate the Intake Process

Often, when people are in the service business, they need certain forms filled out with the client's information prior to doing business. The client will call and be told, "Can you download these forms from our website, print the forms out, fill them in, and bring them back?"

Every step of that process can be automated. In my business, when we take on a client, I don't even talk to the client until they've already done six or eight tasks first. Imagine that: they've never heard of me, they've paid me, they're doing the work, and it's not until after they've done the work that I'll speak to them.

What makes my process work is the short video I made that walks clients through everything they need to do before we can chat. I shot it in a couple of hours, and I never have to explain the process again because it's already there in the video. It shows my clients why they're following that process, and it gets followed all the time.

Action #95: Train Your Clients to Deal with You How You Like

I'm basically training clients in terms of how I want them to deal with me. Right away, I've established that a lot of the process will be done through technology, so they had better learn. If we do the positioning side of things properly, then when the client goes through the intake process, they're excited to deal with us because we've done such a good job. They're not going to have any issues completing that process; they'll go out and learn.

Sit down once and write a script. Make a short video to tell people exactly what you want them to do before you get started. This way, you don't repeat yourself or deal with the hassle of untrained clients. Once it's done, it's done. Your messages won't get mixed up. If you hire somebody, you've created the process and the system, so it never changes.

Action #96: Outsource Everything That You Can

If you're not an expert in web design, then don't try to do it yourself. Bring somebody else on. The same goes for any other field. In the amount of time that it's going to take for you to figure out something new, you could be working on your business, creating and using systems, and charging more clients. Hire somebody to do what you're not an expert at.

If you're looking at doing some internet marketing or Facebook posts or promotions, hire the right people who are experts in what they do, and trust that they're going to do what they've said they're going to do.

Nowadays, there are a lot of people overseas that thrive on freelance work or outsourcing from the North America markets. But it's not as easy as you think. You have to understand how to manage this process, which is a whole book on its own.

I've been outsourcing for 15 or 20 years, and we still have issues sometimes. Get help with that—you can make some very costly mistakes if outsourcing is not done correctly. Find an expert in the field and then delegate the task to them. Ultimately, it can save you a lot of money if it's done right.

Question #25: How Do You Create Stress-Free Freedom for Yourself in Your Business?

People talk about financial freedom and having enough money to do whatever you want to do, but that's only half of it. In my real estate business, I had financial freedom, but it wasn't stress-free freedom. After everything I had done to attain financial freedom, I was still working 80 hours a week, I was still managing 25 people, and I still had $150,000 to $200,000 in overhead to worry about. Sure, I could buy whatever I wanted to whenever I wanted to, but there was still a lot of stress.

We're aiming for a business that gives you that stress-free freedom that I didn't have when I was in real estate. Using these ideas can change the way that you run your business. That includes practices such as training your clients to work with you the way that you want.

Create systems that simplify what you do on a regular basis. Then you can spend less time on your business and more on enjoying your life. We're in business to do the things that we want to do and create the lifestyle that we want. By putting these strategies into play, you'll be able to take more time off and have more time with your family, which creates stress-free freedom. It's all about having that time to spend with your family or loved ones whenever you want.

Action #97: Don't Reinvent the Wheel; Get Mentorship

Why try to do it over? Some people have done what you're doing for 15 or 20 years, as I have. I can give you the quick, easy way of getting things done. I'm a mentor and I have mentors that I work with; we share strategies and ways of establishing things.

I always like to say that I buy the speed that comes from modeling the strategies that people have used to develop their businesses. It works great. You don't have to go to school for five or ten years to learn something before using it. Now, you can learn it over a weekend. That also means you're making money faster. You're not wasting your time on the $10/hour jobs of billing your clients or cleaning the office; you're figuring things out and making your business more profitable.

Action #98: Measure Everything You're Doing against Your Life-by-Design Plan

Once you've created and mapped that ideal lifestyle, look to see whether it's aligned with your ideal lifestyle design plan. If it doesn't match, then you need to work to align it with what you had visualized. Continually look at it, revise it, and ensure that it's contributing to your overall goal.

Many of the concepts that I'm sharing with you are not going to bring change overnight. You have to consistently put the pieces into play on a regular basis. Often, people will drop the ball right in the beginning or somewhere towards the middle. They won't follow through because they were looking for an easy way out, but there is no easy way out that will bring stress-free freedom.

Part of looking at where you're going and how can you get there involves measuring your progress. Determine where you're going to go and how you're going to get there; if your habits and daily activities are not aligning with that, then you need to examine those and make adjustments as needed. Consider using a goal tracker such as LifeTick to set and follow through with your goals.

Action #99: Go to Work Excited Every Day; Reignite the Passion for Your Business

When you're using less time dealing with the usual day-to-day tasks, you're making more money and spending more time with your family. That's what gets you energized and reignites the passion for your business and gets you excited to go to work every single day. Whenever you feel as though you're in a rut, go back to that initial excitement that inspired you to build your business. It's not just about your business, either; it's about the freedom that it brings you to live the good life.

Action #100: Live the Good Life

Now you have the means, money, time, location, and freedom to live the good life. When I left the real estate industry, people would always ask me, "Why did you get out of it? You were doing so well." I said, "Well, I wasn't living the good life."

I had the means, but I didn't have the time or the location freedom (what I mean by "location freedom" is today I can work anywhere in the world). But now, I can go halfway across the world and not miss anything. That's the beauty of creating your own lifestyle.

Think of me as your mentor for creating your ideal business and lifestyle, which gives you the freedom to live the good life. I work with open-minded people who are willing to do what is asked of them. These are business owners in the mid-range of six- or seven-figure incomes.

If you're smart, motivated, and you put ideas into action, you could be on the lower end in terms of income. If you don't have that open mind and aren't open to change, then even if you're on the higher end, you also don't fit in with the criteria. Ultimately, I'm looking for business owners who have an established data-base, are not crazy in debt, and can afford to use the strategies that I provide. If that's you, give me a call. I'd love to hear from you.

Element #5 Conclusion

In this final critical element, we learned how choosing to work on your business instead of working in it can give you incredible results, including the freedom to pursue other interests rather than being chained to your business. You learned how to leverage people, time, and technology, outsourcing lower-paying tasks or those that you are not qualified to do so that you can instead focus your time on projects that bring you the most revenue for your time.

This is truly the start of the stress-free freedom that you have wanted for yourself for so long. Sit back and enjoy it, because you've earned it!

CONCLUSION

You know you've become successful when your business is regularly attracting your ideal clients and you're making plenty of money. What's more, with this book, you've established systems and time-saving processes that give you the space to work on your business rather than in it. You've finally attained the stress-free freedom of enjoying your ideal lifestyle that is supported by your business. Congrats; you've made it!

(Not quite there yet? Give this book another read or two; you'll likely find it even more useful the second time, as different ideas will stand out to you.)

Success doesn't appear out of nowhere. In this book, you discovered these five critical elements that led you through the process of becoming an automated entrepreneur:

- Element #1: Analyze your business and lifestyle

- Element #2: Maximize what makes the most money

- Element #3: Bring in ideal customers

- Element #4: Make money with upsells and cross-sells

- Element #5: Build your dream business

In the first element, you examined the current marketing and cash flow of your business. You looked at your monthly income, what brings in the most revenue, how you can begin attracting your ideal clients, and how becoming the expert and go-to guy in your niche boosts your bottom line.

In the second element, you created a profile of your ideal client and detailed what brings them to your business. You also stepped into their shoes to discover what solutions are optimal for their needs. Then you learned how to differentiate yourself and your offering from the competition, thus revealing your niche's selling points.

In the third element, you figured out how to crush the competition and turn hot prospects into ideal clients who keep coming back. You learned how to put a significant chunk of your business on autopilot so that you can step back from your business and enjoy other aspects of your life. Not only that, but you also discovered the strategies behind building a better customer base, increasing your conversion rate, and simplifying your processes. With a combination of online and offline marketing strategies, you prepared your business to appeal to your target audience of ideal clients.

In the fourth element, you were probably shocked to discover how unbelievably valuable even one of your ideal clients may be. Realizing that worth, however, motivated you to look at your products and services from your clients' perspective, as well as learn how making connections with leaders in different industries can increase the quality of your offering. You also discovered how to build and maintain a strong social media following, among other things.

In the fifth element, you learned the secret to increasing your revenue, only ever dealing with the best of your clients, and spending more time with your family rather than being trapped at your own office. You also discovered how to greatly impact your business and follow a plan that leads to stress-free freedom and being able to live your own ideal lifestyle.

Remember, you can always come back to this book and revisit your favorite pages. I created <u>The Automated Entrepreneur</u> to give my fellow business owners the best playbook to using a multi-dimensional combination of strategies that will cut your expenses in half, double your sales, and provide you a path to ultimately create the ideal lifestyle of which you have always dreamed.

Go to <u>www.BobMangat.com/Book-Offer</u> to get your $693.31 in free money-making resources, spreadsheets, calculators, and more. Plus, get access to a free 30-minute one-on-one consultation with me. It's my gift to you for purchasing this book. If you feel I've wasted your time in the consultation, I'll immediately send you a $250 gift certificate to your favorite restaurant. You have nothing to lose and everything to gain. Now how's that for an irresistable offer? No B.S., just pure results.

Get out there and CRUSH IT!

Bob

Bob

ABOUT THE AUTHOR

My passion is building multimillion-dollar businesses that support my clients' and my ideal lifestyles—not the other way around.

What does an ideal lifestyle mean to me? It means the freedom to work on my own schedule and **never** having to compromise on the most important job in the world: being an attentive husband and a loving father.

Me with my beautiful wife and our two baby boys.

My business and income are strategically designed to empower me to spend time with my family (my beautiful wife and our two amazing boys), pursue other interests and hobbies (playing soccer or coaching my son's soccer team), and also just relax, unwind, and enjoy the fruits of my labor.

*Playing soccer has been one of my favorite
hobbies ever since I was a little kid.*

I wake up every day feeling blessed to be present for our family's most important moments, whether it's our marriage anniversary, my son's birthday, a random Saturday afternoon at the park, or spontaneous vacations and road trips. I treasure all of these happy memories and, thankfully, have not missed a single family event for some time.

But it wasn't always this way. In late 2009, I was driving home a $100,000 Mercedes truck, brand-spanking-new from the dealership. I was stoked.

"Man, I can't believe how far I've come," I said. That year, my real estate business had brought in around $30 million, and I had everything I ever wanted. But when I parked the Mercedes in the garage an hour later and entered the house, my wife and boy weren't there.

I thought, "Is this it? Is this all I'm working for?" Working 80+ hours a week meant missing the first two years of my son's life, and for what? To buy new things? I hated that lonely, empty feeling I got, and I knew this wasn't what I wanted my life to be.

When I was growing up, my parents hadn't spent much time with me because they were working to support our family. I didn't want that for my family. I wanted to be a part of my kids' lives. I had more than I needed, yet I was still working too much. I looked within myself and said, "Where am I going with this? What do I want to do?"

I wanted to spend more time with my family. I wanted to be able to pick up my son at 2:30 from school every single day. I wanted to take him to soccer practice, I wanted to coach his team. Because of my work schedule, I couldn't do any of that, so I shifted my business to make time for my family.

I learned to automate many processes in my business. I gained knowledge by building my business from the ground up and by the things that I started to do. This allowed me to free more time for the interests and people that truly matter to me—all while growing my business and exceeding my income goals.

Nowadays, whenever I meet with and consult for a business owner, I ask that person about their ideal lifestyle. Once I know what their ideal lifestyle is, my team and I create a plan. We look at the client's current lifestyle and discover how much money our client needs to make each month, how many hours they want to work, and every other important factor in creating their ideal lifestyle. Then we set up the business processes to help them live that ideal lifestyle. We reverse engineer everything. We automate the marketing, and we create playbooks, scripts, videos, podcasts, books, and business processes (such as easily training staff with the owner being present).

Many things can be automated. I use technology and systems to give me time to do what I love while providing a better experience overall for my clients. In my real estate business, I was wasting hours on training people. I thought, "Why don't I just build this thing once and let people watch it, and if they have any questions, they can ask me?" So I built the playbook for our business, using this model for every position within our organization. I took a real "set it and forget it" approach.

Today, I build the exact same type of playbooks for chiropractors, pain doctors, weight-loss consultants, and other wellness clinic owners to enhance their businesses for optimal profits and stability... all while creating a structure that supports their ideal lifestyles and allows for plenty of time to spend time with their loved ones.

Speaking in front of a packed house on sales &
marketing automation.

I've written this best-selling book, called "The Automated Entrepreneur," to show you that you can create your ideal lifestyle. This book documents my journey of grinding through 80+ hours of work each week to now working fewer than 20 hours (if that) each week. I did all of that while continuing to bank a very healthy income and pursue other interests—and I've never been happier.